AF651439

THE COMPLEX PROJECT TOOLKIT

Using design thinking to transform the delivery of your hardest projects

KIERAN DUCK

MACMILLAN

In loving memory of Dad, the builder.

First published in 2023 by Major Street Publishing Pty Ltd

First published in India 2023 by Macmillan
an imprint of Pan Macmillan Publishing India Private Limited
707 Kailash Building
26 K. G. Marg, New Delhi 110001
www.panmacmillan.co.in

Pan Macmillan, The Smithson, 6 Briset Street, Farringdon, London EC1M 5NR
Associated companies throughout the world
www.panmacmillan.com

ISBN 978-81-963653-7-0

Copyright © Kieran Duck 2023

The moral rights of the author have been asserted.

All rights reserved. No part of this publication may be reproduced, stored in or introduced into a retrieval system, or transmitted, in any form, or by any means (electronic, mechanical, photocopying, recording or otherwise) without the prior written permission of the publisher. Any person who does any unauthorized act in relation to this publication may be liable to criminal prosecution and civil claims for damages.

1 3 5 7 9 8 6 4 2

Internal design by Production Works
Printed and bound in India by Replika Press Pvt. Ltd.

This book is sold subject to the condition that it shall not, by way of trade or otherwise, be lent, hired out, or otherwise circulated without the publisher's prior consent in any form of binding or cover other than that in which it is published and without a similar condition including this condition being imposed on the subsequent purchaser.

CONTENTS

INTRODUCTION

The first time it struck me that the standard project management toolkit was incomplete for complex projects was ten years ago. I was standing outside a restaurant in the northern suburbs of Sydney, engaged in one of those deep conversations that start late in the evening.

I had just finished dinner with the leadership team of a multi-billion-dollar infrastructure project. The project was running late, had missed a couple of major milestones and was only a few months away from the final design sign-off, which looked like it would be delayed as well. We were pushing to get it back on track, and this dinner was my first chance to bring the whole leadership team together in a social setting.

As the evening wound down and the team started to disperse, I found myself talking with Sean, the project administrator. Sean was a master of the project toolkit. On all the projects I'd worked on over the years, I'd never met anyone as capable with project analytics and tracking. He maintained all the project plans, the resource models and the risk registers, and also ran detailed earned value and stochastic modelling that provided insight and control over the project.

As the last of the team drifted away, Sean confided in me that he had a problem. Before this dinner, his analysis had put the probability of on-time achievement of the final design milestone at less than 1%. Now he believed that the time we had just spent together as a team had lifted the probability of success closer to 10%, but he had no idea how to work that into his projections. He didn't know how to model it. He couldn't prove it, but he did believe it.

Two thoughts stood out for me that evening. The first was the realisation that rigorously applying the standard project management process, even though Sean was an extremely competent practitioner of the science, had not been enough to guarantee success. The second was a question: if calculating the probability of a project's success makes no allowance for the level of connection within the team, which clearly impacts performance, what else is missing from the standard toolkit?

After that dinner I continued to see experienced managers struggling with complex projects. They would put in long hours but never get ahead of the situation. They would be dragged into detailed discussions on convoluted topics and be surprised when decisions were changed. Their teams would complain that the plan was never going to be delivered and that no one wanted to hear that.

Most of these project managers had strong technical backgrounds, which had driven success in large, technically complicated projects. However, in complexity – where there is no clear path forward and lots of different opinions at play – they had reached the limit of their toolkit. Despite decades of experience, they were constantly frustrated and ineffective.

It wasn't that they were no good at project management. They had a lot to offer and brought great processes for normal operations, but they weren't seeing and addressing the heart of the problem when it came to complexity. They just didn't have the extra gears they needed for the situation – like taking your two-wheel-drive car off-road, where you might make progress but encounter lots of issues. These managers needed a low-range four-wheel-drive for some of the rugged terrain they were navigating.

From this realisation was born the idea of extending the project toolkit to better handle complexity.

The standard project management toolkit provides a straightforward instruction manual for delivery success – or at least, that is how it appears. Unfortunately, when it comes to complexity, the well-known methods produce the exact opposite of what you would expect: detailed analysis creates confusion rather than clarity; plans designed to lay out the path forward constantly change; decisions intended to create certainty and move everyone forward get revisited. The promise of reliability and control breaks down in the face of complexity. Instead of improving the chance of success, the standard approach exacerbates the problems it is meant to counter.

At the heart of this dilemma is the fact that complex projects are fundamentally creative and emergent endeavours, and we fail when we approach them with the standard toolkit based on an analytical way of thinking. We need a different mental model to succeed in complexity. We may love the illusion of predictability and control that comes from detailed plans and coloured status reports, but when the project has lots of unknowns, these artefacts provide false hope and draw attention to the wrong things, reducing the chance of success.

Traditional project management grew up in a different time. It has an industrial heritage, focused on coordinating a large number of resources to deliver an outcome with certainty, and underpinned significant advances over centuries. In the last few decades project management has expanded, with methods like Agile being used to cope with unclear or changing requirements. These methods work when the answer is known but the details haven't been worked out. Large-scale system implementations, which once had a low chance of success, now have a common method.

But more recently there has been a significant shift in the nature of our most valuable projects. Those that deliver real advantage and transform the way we operate are characterised by a high level of emergence, unknowns and opinions.

To succeed in this complexity we need to revisit some of the basic principles, such as the need for certainty and predictability. How do you set a deadline when your major transformation program depends on support from a number of employee groups with their own agendas? And if you do set a deadline, what does it mean when your status report goes from green to yellow to red within weeks because of information you only became aware of along the way?

The standard project toolkit is not set up for this, and the result is that complex projects often fail. When we try to force control on an evolving situation, we create confusion and mistrust, leaving team members frustrated and demotivated. Our inability to deliver in complexity curtails our ambition, leading us to prefer safe options rather than game-changing advances.

We need an enhanced approach to managing complex projects – one that draws from those who operate in ambiguity and emergence every day. The best source of this is the minds of designers. Designers spend their time creating new concepts, ideas and products. They are experts at responding to the ambiguous world around them. This book takes lessons from the way designers think and describes an extended project toolkit that improves the delivery of complex projects. It is not about throwing out all we know about project management, but rather enhancing what exists.

First, we have to realise that complex projects are a different type of problem. They are connected, subjective, unknowable, unique and constrained – and these five characteristics set them apart from projects that are just technically complicated. Understanding this, the inherent difficulty in meeting project management's need for predictability and certainty becomes obvious. This explains why the 'best practice' responses to project issues don't work and why the standard approach can, at best, only provide a dangerous illusion of control and progress in emergent situations.

The Complex Project Toolkit creates a new framing of complex project delivery based on these characteristics of complexity. It is a guide to how to deliver the best results within ambiguity. This toolkit takes a holistic approach, covering mindsets, practices and skills. The mindset change is about a fundamental shift in our relationship with certainty and different attitudes to experimentation and 'failure'. It is about embracing ambiguity, giving up knowing the answer and being open to the ideas of others. Six mindsets and their resulting behaviours are described that introduce new concepts to project management, such as 'Always curious' and 'Choose your own path'.

At the heart of the Complex Project Toolkit are new practices. These are not 'paint-by-number' prescriptive processes to be blindly applied. They represent an overall framework for how to approach the paradoxes inherent in complex projects: the need to move forward while maintaining the space to think through emerging issues, and the need to understand and incorporate opinions while finalising an answer and delivering a result. Holding all of this together is the belief by the team that the outcome is worthwhile.

Rounding out the toolkit is an enhanced skill set that supports the new practices and draws heavily from the capabilities of designers. More than whiteboards and Post-it notes, it is a specific set of skills that can be learned and applied. The skill-set includes conversation, sense-making and adaption.

I've seen first-hand how a purely scientific approach to complex projects reduces the probability of success and exhausts everyone involved. I have also seen the Complex Project Toolkit lift performance and drive teams to succeed. I have experienced projects in deep trouble being rescued when the conventional project managers opened their minds and developed new skills. I have worked with teams that have lifted both their performance and satisfaction in the project. While many effective project managers practise some of these techniques already, in this book I lay out the whole toolkit so it can be understood, taught and replicated.

This book covers a lot of ground – from building trains, to special forces training, to impacting wilderness areas in the name of progress. It includes stories of significant project turnarounds and personal development that fundamentally shifted the enjoyment people took from their roles in very challenging situations. The stories have been recreated from memory and names have been changed to provide anonymity. Some situations have been combined to make a point in a more succinct way.

This book is for anyone who wants to make sense of project complexity and understand how to lead from a different place, shift the way teams operate, and raise the level of performance and ownership in complex projects.

Part I

THE PROBLEM WITH COMPLEXITY

Chapter I
THE EVOLUTION OF PROJECT MANAGEMENT

'Nothing is particularly hard if you divide it into small jobs.'
—Henry Ford

The Empire State Building was not only the tallest building in the world when completed: it also represented the state of the art in coordinating vast numbers of people and massive amounts of materials.

Located at the corner of 34th St and 5th Ave in New York, it was specifically designed to be the tallest building in the world. It was backed by investment from General Motors, who wanted to eclipse the nearby Chrysler Building, which was also under construction. After six months of planning by architecture firm Shreve, Lamb & Harmon, groundworks started on St Patrick's Day, 1930.

Starrett Brothers and Eken won the contract to build the new structure. As one of the leading companies for constructing skyscrapers, they were an obvious choice. They had the experience working with steel frames, but more importantly, they had expertise in programming the work and coordinating all the materials and the effort of the 3000 people who would be employed on the site.

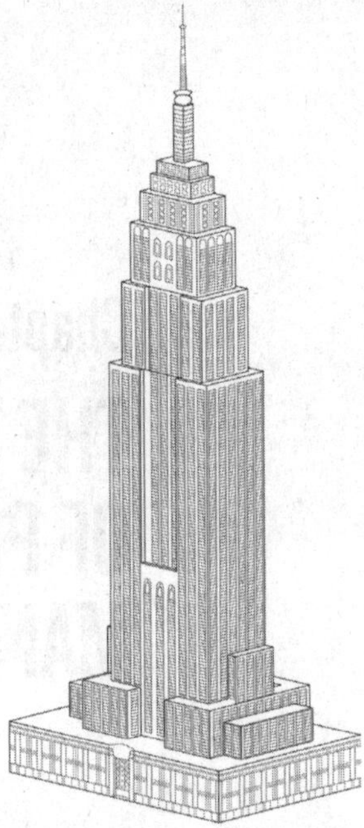

The construction proceeded at a fantastic pace. In one ten-day period the building added fourteen floors. This achievement was made possible by tightly coordinating deliveries of up to 200 trucks per day in the middle of the teeming city. With very little storage room on site, timing of deliveries and every activity in the supply chain was closely managed. There are stories of the logistics being so finely tuned that steel was turning up at the site still warm from the mill in Pittsburgh. Through tight control the entire building was finished in 410 days, two weeks ahead of schedule, at a rate that would be difficult to match today.

It was all about scale

This is what the standard project management model was made for: delivering industrial-scale outcomes with confidence and control. This model is about coordinating a vast array of resources and people to deliver reliable results on time and on budget through strong process control.

While evidence of project management can be found as far back as in ancient Egypt, the formalised practices took a big leap forward in the early 20th century to underpin the increase in engineering projects such as railways, bridges, ships and buildings. The profound questions of the time centred on reliability: How do you get materials to turn up at the right time? How do you coordinate the efforts of hundreds of people? How do you predict whether the work will be completed on time? The focus was on creating massive objects at speed. Artisanal or bespoke techniques were never going to deliver results on the scale required.

The 1950s saw the expansion of project management techniques. Critical path analysis reduced project duration and resource usage, PERT charts managed dependencies and earned value analysis confirmed a project was progressing as planned. All of these techniques focused on analysis and forecasting to meet three goals: optimal resource usage, predictable timeframes and quality control. This scientific perspective underpins project management as we know it today.

The resulting toolkit

The standard project management approach is designed to create certainty in project delivery. There is a clear path to success. It starts with writing a scope document or project charter to define the objectives, deliverables and overall approach, drawing on the experience of the project manager to set the standard. This is followed by all the supporting infrastructure: a governance committee with clear roles and accountability to maintain tight control over the project; risk management sessions to identify and mitigate potential issues; and regular status reports to show which areas need attention. Stakeholders are identified and managed. Benefits are defined and tracked against the original promise.

The standard approach to project management is built on the tried and tested mindsets listed in Table 1.1 overleaf.

Using this paradigm, the best project managers are rigorous and analytical. They know all the details of the contract. They bring experience from other projects to bear on this situation.

They are good at managing stakeholders and always deliver status reports on time. Their role is that of a traffic controller, coordinating all the moving parts to ensure outputs are delivered on time and to specification. Certainty is preferred and kudos is given to those who can deliver exactly what was asked for.

This standard project approach has delivered many project successes. But then information technology projects came along, and things started to go wrong.

Table 1.1: Standard project management mindsets

Mindset	Description
Focus on **what** needs to be delivered.	Once the project is approved, deliver what was asked for. Focus on the objective and progress towards that result.
Find an **expert** to define the approach.	What worked before will work again. Find people who have done this before and draw on their expertise.
Documents and plans are critical.	A rigorous, agreed project plan is at the heart of performance. If in doubt, refer to the contract.
Control the process to remove uncertainty.	Manage risks to reduce uncertainty. Follow the process to ensure reliability.
More **detail** provides greater understanding.	If anything is unclear, break it down into its component pieces to provide clarity.
Minimise the level of change once underway.	Any change makes it hard to deliver on the original plan, so keep it to a minimum.

The world moved on

Technology got in the way

In the late 1980s the Australian bank Westpac embarked on a substantial project to replace its core banking system. The project was called CS90. By 1992 the project was closed and the company took a $150 million loss.[1] In 1993, FoxMeyer was one of the largest distributors of pharmaceuticals in the US and the first major pharmaceutical distribution company to undertake a large-scale enterprise resource planning (ERP) replacement. At the time, it had sales of US$5 billion, shipping around 500,000 items a day. Three years later, following the massive failure of the project, with costs blowing out to over $100 million, the company was bankrupt and sold to a competitor for US$80 million.[2]

Despite everything that was known about project management, large-scale technology projects were failing. The world had changed. More and more projects involved building invisible software rather than physical structures. This new kind of project was beyond the experience of most executives. They didn't know how to tell if progress was being made and were often surprised when their multi-year development was either a massive failure or superseded by a software package available in the market at a fraction of the cost. For project managers, this was a whole new game.

The toolkit was adjusted

Project management had a new set of questions to answer. How do I manage progress when progress isn't visible to everyone? How do I know what I want until I see what I can get? If the outcome can be changed in a few hours with a few keystrokes, how do I stop people changing their mind about the design? How do I ensure the new system will be used by people who have no experience with computers?

New project management techniques were introduced to deal with the flexibility and configuration options offered by new technologies. More iterative models such as Spiral and Agile were developed. These methods allowed the project's requirements to be refined as prototypes were created, or segments of functionality were delivered, and understanding improved. Change management techniques arose to deal with the disconnect between those who built the product and those who had to use it. The project manager's role expanded from just organising resources to also ensuring that stakeholders were managed and understood what was being delivered.

Throughout these adjustments to the project management approach, the underlying mindsets remained relatively unchanged. Changes to specific design elements were allowed within the tightly defined scope of the project.

The focus of these new methods remained on systematic control to increase the certainty of delivering what was promised. A fundamental assumption of these methods is that the outcome of the project is clear and agreed upon. But what happens when you can't agree on the project objective?

The rise of complexity

The Snowy River, located in south-east Australia, has its source in the country's highest mountains. Fed by melting snow and rainfall along its course, the river flows through rugged bushland and coastal plains to the Tasman Sea in the south. In the 1940s, plans were developed to utilise the water of the Snowy by turning the river inland to support the burgeoning agricultural areas of the Murray and Murrumbidgee Valleys. As the plans developed, the idea of also generating hydroelectric power to meet the needs of a growing population was added. In 1949 work started on the Snowy Mountains Scheme. The construction of 16 dams, 3 reservoirs, 7 power stations and 145 kilometres of pipes redirected most of the water flow to irrigate arid inland areas and produce electricity on the way.[3] Roads and railways were cut through pristine wilderness areas of the Kosciuszko National Park to support the massive endeavour.

This was the largest engineering project in Australia's history, and a country of only seven million people was going to need some help to build it. Expertise in heavy engineering and operating in alpine regions was brought in from overseas to drive the project. Two-thirds of the workforce were immigrants from more than 30 countries, many escaping war-torn Europe. To accommodate the workers over the life of the operations, more than 100 temporary camps and seven towns were constructed, two of which – Cabramurra and Khancoban – remain to this day.

But other towns had to be moved. Jindabyne had been established in 1840 on the banks of the Snowy River and served as a major river crossing.[4] The construction of the Jindabyne dam would result in the entire town being submerged in one of the new reservoirs. So, in the 1960s the town was moved a couple of kilometres to its present site, on the shore of Lake Jindabyne. It was a similar story for Adaminaby and Talbingo. Some residents were keen to move into new houses with modern facilities and comforts; others were sad to see their old township disappear but understood they couldn't stand in the way of progress.

Completed on time in 1974, the entire program was delivered within budget. When fully commissioned, the seven power stations had a capacity of 4100 megawatts and increased the output of the largest agricultural area in the country.

It was heralded as a resounding success both in infrastructure project delivery and in building the capability of a nation. It is regarded as a 'world-class civil engineering project' by the American Society of Civil Engineers and is listed as a National Engineering Landmark by Engineers Australia as part of its Engineering Heritage Recognition Program.[5, 6]

Clearly the Snowy Mountains Scheme was a huge success by all standard measures of project management. However, over the years a problem became apparent.

The redirection of water inland meant that flows in the Snowy River downstream from the dams had drastically reduced, and the river was dying. The change was so dramatic that often the river ran dry, which had a devastating effect on the habitats of platypuses and Australian bass. The original scheme had been based on the nation's power needs and the dream of building an agricultural region through irrigation, with little regard for the ecological impacts.

An extensive public campaign in the 1990s voiced concern over this. State elections in nearby districts were fought and won over the issue of water flows in the Snowy River. In 2000 the state governments of New South Wales and Victoria agreed to increase flows by a target of 28%, and to pay compensation to the inland farms that would have reduced flows. In 2002 the target was adjusted to 21%. It was first hit in 2017, meaning it took almost as long to reach agreement and restore the flows as it took to build the entire scheme.[7]

Projects have changed

This example demonstrates how projects are different now. The objective is no longer just to get something built – you also need to take into account a wide range of perspectives and potential impacts. If you were to take on the original Snowy Mountains Scheme today, the complexity would be much higher than when it first started. The biggest issue to deal with in the 1950s was how to get enough workers into the country and where to house them during construction. These days the concerns would revolve around the political and economic implications of importing a foreign labour force, the impact of relocating townships and the environmental impact on the habitat of the platypus. Seventy years ago the problem was one of scale; now much of the project complexity comes from all the different perspectives that need to be considered.

This change is happening all over the world. In the late 1990s Vietnam developed plans to build dams and hydroelectric power stations on the Dong Nai River to supply power to meet the country's growing energy needs. Despite significant opposition and the displacement of thousands of people, construction started on the Dai Ninh dam in 2001 and it was commissioned in 2008. This dam was part of a large series of dams for the river. Only five years later, however, in 2013, two further dams (6 and 6a) were cancelled due to environmental concerns and international pressure. Many of the arguments against the dams were the same as those for previous constructions that had proceeded, including 'changing hydrological dynamics, loss of riparian ecosystems, blocking of fish migration routes, loss of aquatic species and habitat, displacement of locals...', but this time the opposition was successful.[8, 9]

The next chapter defines the characteristics of a complex project, but for the moment just think of them as those projects that involve a lot of opinions and a lot of unknowns, and often unintended consequences – they can be business transformations, innovation programs or even large infrastructure projects with many connected parts. The boundary of what is in and out of scope can be unclear at the beginning, and even the definition of what deliverables are required can depend on how the project evolves.

Complex projects can face situations with distributed power that play havoc with your plan. For example, imagine a large bank has decided that to remain competitive they have to shift their business dramatically towards a greater use of online technology and fewer frontline bankers. The plan is to exit 2000 operational staff and hire 1000 IT people. Managers put their plan together and step into the process of making the change. Then all the staff react, deciding they won't support the change and announcing they will challenge it in court. What has your timeline become? Your nine-month plan to deliver all these changes just became eighteen months or longer of drawn-out consultation. The timing now depends on how long it takes to reach an agreement.

The complexity of a project is driven by the context in which it operates, not the technical nature of the project. Having said that, technical projects can be complex. Constructing a bridge is an industrial undertaking, but the argument about how the increased traffic flow will affect the local community is one of the elements that can make it complex. Building submarines is technically complicated, using materials that are difficult to work with – systems and sensors that operate at the limit of our understanding of the physics of seawater – but the complexity is created by the fact that it is being built by a consortium of companies with different cultures and motivations. Working beyond the boundary of a single organisation adds complexity because it requires all participants to contribute as agreed and to operate in a way that is best for the entire project rather than just in their self-interest.

The reality is that the most valuable projects are dripping with complexity, either driven by unknowns or the increasing number of voices involved. How do you set a reliable budget for a genuine innovation that no one has attempted before? How do you create certainty when there are so many opinions involved? What do you do when a social media campaign stops your development project? How do you put together a reliable project plan with so many unknowns? You can make an educated guess, but the outcomes will always depend on what happens day to day.

Complex projects have dilemmas and difficult trade-offs at their cores. Is it better to exit 2000 staff and change the business, or keep those roles and potentially risk the livelihoods of the 10,000 that would remain? Is it better to flood a wilderness and a few villages to provide consistent, carbon-neutral hydroelectricity, or to build new coal-fired power plants in the face of climate change? These are the types of dilemmas that occur in complexity.

Ineffective responses

There is also a paradox that arises when you apply the standard project management toolkit to solve issues in complex projects – the situation doesn't respond to interventions the way you expect it to. The responses designed to bring everything back on track create the opposite results to what was intended:

- Demands for 'quick wins' lock in choices that have unpredictable impacts later in the project and reduce the value delivered.
- Focusing on getting one thing done well creates surprises elsewhere because everything is so interconnected.
- Diving into detail doesn't create clarity; instead it sows confusion and distrust as it highlights more and more unknowns.
- Being decisive slows down the project and wastes effort because choices are revisited as new information comes to light.

All of these reactions might be considered best practice, but they come at the situation with an ineffective mindset and don't address the heart of the complexity. Chapter 4 explains how the way of thinking that underpins the standard approach is fundamentally misaligned with the nature of complexity. This explains why complexity can leave experienced project managers feeling overwhelmed and out of their depth – not that they will tell anyone this. Complex projects are difficult, with tight deadlines and many unknowns, and you don't need to make them worse by turning up with the wrong mental model.

All of this leads to the question: if the normal project toolkit has such significant downsides, why are these actions repeated day after day? Because the normal approach works for projects that aren't complex. However, when you approach complexity in the standard way and try to create certainty where it doesn't exist, you exhaust the team and kill off any chance of a successful result.

It is worth improving

The ability to deliver complex projects is a valuable advantage. Low-growth environments and new business models are driving organisations to take on more complex projects, such as high-risk innovations or business transformations.

Generally, performance in complex projects is poor. Research by the Helmsman Institute has shown there is 'an exponential reduction in performance above a complexity threshold'.[10] So as project complexity increases, the chance of success falls.

But the problem is much broader than project failures. Sometimes the failures are large and obvious, making headline news and putting the viability of companies at risk, but the vast majority of breakdowns are not so sensational. It is common for projects to fall short of expectations (in a study by Brightline of companies with annual revenues of $1 billion or more, '90% of companies failed to meet strategic objectives because they don't implement well'[11]). It is also common for projects to take longer than hoped and ignore obvious problems – and then require heroic efforts by a few individuals to recover them. These valiant recoveries are common, hard to detect and rarely discussed. The impact on business results is more obvious and easier to measure than the impact on people.

Olivia, a very experienced program manager, was leading a workstream in a large business transformation. She was responsible for reporting to the program office and was required to submit updated project plans every month. The integrated nature of the transformation meant that her workstream was waiting for resolution of an industrial relations issue before moving to implementation. As long as this issue remained unresolved, her workstream was on hold, delaying any future delivery. Despite the recognition of this uncertainty, the program office required an updated plan every month based on current assumptions. She was expending effort redoing the project plan every few weeks, knowing it was a waste of time because the dates weren't real and would need to be revised when broader issue was resolved.

Not only did this mean Olivia felt like she was wasting her time, she was left frustrated with the way the whole program operated and questioning why she was spending months running around in circles. The situation demoralised and demotivated her, and she wanted to get out.

It is not uncommon for complex projects to frustrate staff when the standard approach to projects is used. John was a long-time employee of an insurance firm involved in a transformation. He was passionate about making sure the change worked for the organisation he knew so well. However, when he highlighted issues with an approach or flaw in the design, he was dismissed as a naysayer and regarded as a roadblock. He found that in the push to stick to deadlines, his concerns were ignored, and he felt discarded. Instead of sitting back and waiting for his predictions to come true, taking satisfaction in being right, he demeaned and complained about the project to anyone who would listen. This negative energy made it worse for everyone involved.

Not listening to the voice of experience and pushing ahead with an approach that doesn't fit the situation are some of the symptoms of blindly applying the standard toolkit in a complex situation. This leaves teams exhausted and wounded, and leaders wondering what more they could've done.

Unfortunately, many people can recount stories of a horror project – the time they put in long hours and huge amounts of energy only to be left burnt out and frustrated by the stress and demands of the situation. It's not just workload that makes these projects difficult. Some of the best projects I've worked on involved long hours, late nights and tight deadlines, but they were creative and built something special. Most people don't mind working hard on a problem when they are clear on the purpose of their endeavours and their effort is respected.

A way forward

In his book *A Whole New Mind*, Daniel H. Pink describes the movement from the Agricultural Age (farmers) to the Industrial Age (factory workers), through the Information Age (knowledge workers) to the Conceptual Age (creators and empathisers). Project management grew up in the Industrial Age, has adjusted to meet the requirements of the Information Age and now faces the challenge of moving into the Conceptual Age, which 'involves the ability to empathise, to understand the subtleties of human interaction'.[12] This is where the standard toolkit comes up short. An extended project management approach that genuinely addresses complexity has to put this concept of 'human interaction' at its core.

A shift in performance is not going to come from simply adding a few extra steps to the plan or an additional workshop to 'get everyone on the same page'. The Complex Project Toolkit, presented in Part 2 of this book, brings forward a whole new system of mindsets, practices and skills for delivering in complexity which has been successful in complex projects. By using these techniques, teams have been able to completely redesign their project approach, build stronger connections, focus on the things that really matter and deliver the difficult outcomes. One project accelerated a major milestone by six months, along with the payment worth tens of millions of dollars, providing a significant cash injection to the business earlier than forecasted.

Over the years, project management has evolved to meet the different challenges that projects encounter. The issue we face now is that while the nature of projects is changing, the project management toolkit hasn't kept pace with this change. To find a way through, first we need to understand the nature of complexity. The next chapter lays out the five characteristics that define complexity, which will provide an insight into why a new toolkit is required.

Chapter 2
THE NATURE OF COMPLEXITY

'Nothing is perfect. Life is messy.
Relationships are complex.
Outcomes are uncertain.
People are irrational.'
—Hugh Mackay

Complex projects have five characteristics that set them apart from normal projects. Each of these characteristics provides an insight into why the standard project toolkit, with its focus on predictability and control, struggles with complexity. Understanding these characteristics makes it possible to distinguish between a technically complicated project and a complex one, and to see why a new way of operating is required. Complexity is never constant, rising as more issues emerge and falling as they are overcome. But first let me be clear on what I mean by 'project'.

Complex projects create something new

A 'project' can be defined as an activity with a defined start and end, a clear outcome and allocated resources; but this definition is too simple when talking about complexity. For example, when an airline introduces a new type of aircraft, a huge effort is required before taking delivery of the first plane. The project needs to design the internal layout, train pilots and cabin crew, arrange maintenance and support equipment, and bring together all the other elements required to make the launch a success. The delivery of the second aircraft also meets the formal definition of a project with defined start, end, outcome and resources, but it is much less complex because many of the decisions have already been made. So it is with the third aircraft, and the fourth, and so on. After a few have been delivered, the process is well templated, and while the activity can still be formally classified as a 'project', it is much less complex.

Complex projects can be distinguished by the way they deal with problems not yet solved and create something new or unique. They are how you introduce a change to the world, how you explore different frontiers, how you execute business strategy and how you create a different future. It is not just exploiting what you know; it is opening up a new way of working with unions, or setting up a business in a country where you have never operated, or building more buses than you have ever done before with a new global supply chain. It is important to be clear on what separates a complex project from a simple one.

Five characteristics of complexity

There are many definitions of complexity. Complex projects have been described as 'characterized by uncertainty, ambiguity, dynamic interfaces, and significant political or external influences'.[1] Some models portray the level of detailed technical requirements as driving complexity, but this makes projects complicated rather than complex – more on that distinction later. The commonly used Turner and Cochrane model of complex projects defines complexity as having undefined goals and methods.[2] More recent models, such as the Global Alliance for the Project Professions (GAPPS) Aitken-Carnegie-Duncan Complexity Table (ACDC) and the International Project Management Association (IPMA) Complexity model, contain extensive lists of elements that explain the level of uncertainty and management challenges in the project – from the number of involved parties to the level of reporting and the strategic importance of the outcomes.[3, 4]

While useful in creating clarity about the situation, many of these models don't differentiate between shortcomings in project processes and the inherent nature of complexity, which exists even if strong processes are in place. For example, if there is uncertainty in project funding, is it caused by a problem in the way money is allocated or is it based on unreconciled conflicting views on the value of doing the project? The first can be fixed by using standard project management methods to address any process gaps, while the other requires a deeper understanding of why the differing views exist.

It is this second type of breakdown, which is rooted in the social constructs of a project, that project managers often downplay or miss in favour of putting in place consistent processes. But they do so at their own peril. Understanding the dynamics of this socially driven complexity, and realising how we need to extend the project toolkit, is the focus of this book. My experience and research have revealed five characteristics that define the nature of this complexity, shown in Figure 2.1 over the page.

These characteristics overlap and combine to confound the analytical nature of the existing project toolkit and put complex projects at risk. Understanding these characteristics makes it clear that the standard approach has gaps and drives us to reframe how we approach projects.

Figure 2.1: Five characteristics of complexity

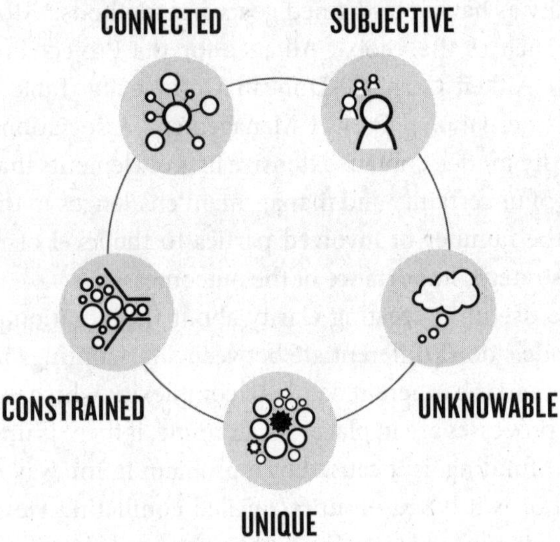

Connected

You have probably heard the Indian parable about the blind men who encounter an elephant for the first time. Each touches a different part of the animal – the tail, the trunk, an ear, a leg, a tusk. Their understanding is limited by the evidence they have before them. As each arrives at his own interpretation based on his partial experience, there is much disagreement about what it is they are describing. In some versions of the story, the disagreement between them leads to distrust and conflict. They assume their partial experience explains the whole and ignore the experience of others.

People operating in complex projects are like these blind men: no single person can see the entire system because there are so many elements and connections that are beyond their purview. This leads to issues that confound the standard project management approach.

Unseen consequences

The most significant implication of connectedness, where no single person can see the whole system, is that there will be consequences you didn't expect.

Launched in 2010, the Airbus A320neo is a more fuel-efficient version of Airbus's top-selling A320 family of aircraft. One of the main selling points of the A320neo was that it had the same type rating as the earlier versions of the A320. This meant pilots didn't need extensive training on the new aircraft, ground handling equipment was common and it was relatively inexpensive to introduce the new aircraft into an airline. To counter this move, Boeing offered a more efficient version of their 737 narrow-body aircraft, the Boeing 737 MAX, with redesigned wings and larger engines. Announced in 2011, Boeing promised that the aircraft would also maintain the same type rating as the original 737 so that adoption of the new aircraft into existing fleets would be seamless.

To maintain the same type rating on the 737 MAX, the design had to lie within the original 1968 FAA certification of the type. However, the new, larger engines changed the aircraft's flight dynamics, which could stall the aircraft in certain conditions. This effect was offset by new software that would react to potential problems and adjust the aircraft controls. The intent was to ensure the same flight characteristics as previous models. But the system used only limited sensors to provide the necessary flight data, making the aircraft susceptible to problems if the sensors failed. When one did fail the result was a situation that, in the hands of inexperienced pilots, led to two fatal crashes and the worldwide grounding of the aircraft.[5]

No single person was in a position to see that the desire to maintain similarity in type certification would lead to technical issues that would tragically kill hundreds of people and ground the aircraft for 20 months.

Fuzzy boundary

The boundary of a complex project is arbitrary, and you need to make a call on where to draw the line.

When a supermarket chain sets about transforming their business, they have to decide how far into their suppliers' business they are going to reach. Will they require these external organisations to implement new systems and processes? Do the suppliers need to retrain all their staff? Does the completion of the project rely on all suppliers meeting all their obligations? No matter where you draw the boundary, there will always be questions about the benefits of going further and the associated time and cost trade-offs. This fuzziness can cause havoc when trying to lock down scope, and it's not unusual for these limits to be revised as the project progresses and the reality of the situation is understood.

Hard to slice it into pieces

All of the connections within a complex situation make it difficult to find clear boundaries between the elements of the project.

Large projects are normally divided into workstreams for the purpose of assigning and tracking accountability. If you have ever done this, you will know that drawing boundaries is as much art as science. The workstreams always need to work together because complex projects are a holism in which the components alone don't deliver the final result. When you set up the workstreams there is always overlap between them, and any attempt to treat them as distinct pieces loses sight of the nuances of the situation.

Complexity has been described by some scholars as the inability of a single language or perspective to describe all the properties of the system being observed. Therefore, to understand a complex situation, you need multiple languages and perspectives. If you can't know everything, then you have to rely on others for content and context.

The connected nature of complexity starts to explain why a new toolkit is required. Defining scope requires clear boundaries.

Work breakdown structures in project plans rely on a reductionist approach to the topic and ignore overlaps and nuances. Tracking benefits is difficult in complexity because the drivers can't be isolated from all the other changes going on. And when one person can't see the whole system, the 'project manager as expert' model no longer fits.

The dilemma is that you can't slice the project into chunks and treat each as separate and sterile, because the interactions are significant; but at the same time, if you leave the project whole there is too much breadth to cover for team members to be effective. You need a layered approach with an overall picture – a map of the complete territory, where team members can see their role and also the connections to the other parts of the system. Creating this approach takes time and judgement and needs to bring together multiple perspectives from different areas of the project.

Subjective

In the final scene of the 1994 movie *Pulp Fiction*, Jules and Vincent, the main characters of the film, are sitting in a diner discussing the events of the day and how they narrowly escaped being killed by an inept gunman. Jules describes it as 'the miracle we witnessed', to which Vincent replies, 'The miracle you witnessed. I witnessed a freak occurrence.' Jules goes on to describe how he is going to fundamentally change his life, how he is going to 'walk the Earth' and 'just be Jules'. The incident had no impact on Vincent.[6] How is it possible that they experienced exactly the same situation but had such different interpretations of it?

The COVID-19 outbreak in 2020 was similar. Other than during the first few outbreaks, all countries had the same information and saw the effects in a variety of situations, yet they headed down distinctly different paths when addressing the pandemic. Even within cities, different companies, organisations and individuals had different reactions to the outbreak.

Complex projects are full of situations like this, in which exactly the same information prompts completely different conclusions. So how do we frame a situation when there is no 'external truth' we can call on for the right answer?

Wicked versus tame problems

In 1973, Horst Rittel and Melvin Webber wrote a paper called 'Dilemmas in a General Theory of Planning'.[7] The real significance of this paper has nothing to do with the town planning problem they were trying to solve; rather, it is in how it distinguished the nature of the problem they found themselves engaged in. In particular, they coined the terms 'tame' and 'wicked' problems.

A broken copy machine is a tame problem. We all agree it is broken; there is no debate here – clearly it has stopped working. There is a diagnostic process to find the source of the problem and make sure the correct issue is addressed. We can also agree when the machine is fixed and working again. The imperative in a tame problem is getting it solved as efficiently as possible.

Wicked problems are not like this. They involve questions like: What's the best way to deliver this project on time? What is the best tax policy for the country? How do we address world hunger? They are difficult to solve because of incomplete, contradictory or changing requirements that are often difficult to recognise. Sometimes we can't even agree there is a problem to be solved. Wicked problems depend on your world view. They are social rather than technical, and the greater the number of points of view on the topic, the greater the wickedness.

Complex projects are wicked problems in one form or another. Rittel and Webber identified ten dimensions of wicked problems (see Box A opposite), and while there is insight in the whole list, I want to focus on a few in particular.

A: Dilemmas in a general theory of planning

When trying to define guidelines for ideal social policy, specifically in relation to town planning, Rittel and Webber found there was an issue with the pervading focus of structured approaches to goal definition, forecasting and the 'cybernetic process of governance'. They began to realise that 'one of the most intractable problems is that of defining problems', at which point they identified two types of problems – tame and wicked. Tame problems were easily accommodated by the current analytical approaches, but wicked problems had ten traits that made this approach ineffective:

1. There is no definitive formulation of a wicked problem.
2. Wicked problems have no stopping rule.
3. Solutions to wicked problems are not true-or-false but good-or-bad.
4. There is no immediate and no ultimate test of a solution to a wicked problem.
5. Every solution to a wicked problem is a 'one-shot operation'; because there is no opportunity to learn by trial-and-error, every attempt counts significantly.
6. Wicked problems do not have an enumerable (or extensively describable) set of potential solutions, nor is there a well-described set of permissible operations that may be incorporated into the plan.
7. Every wicked problem is essentially unique.
8. Every wicked problem can be considered to be a symptom of another problem.
9. The existence of a discrepancy in representing a wicked problem can be explained in numerous ways. The choice of explanation determines the nature of the problem's resolution.
10. The planner has no right to be wrong.

The significance of your world view

The first trait of a wicked problem is: 'There is no definitive formulation of a wicked problem.'

Have you noticed how the classification of a problem depends on the background of the person you ask? If you have HR look at the issue, it will be a cultural or training problem; ask finance and it requires an activity-based cost approach; the change manager sees a complete lack of communication; the project manager insists we just need a more structured approach. And they may all be right.

How you define a wicked problem depends on your opinion. This opinion depends on your world view, which is how you interpret the world and is shaped by the combination of all your experiences to this point in your life. In the article 'The Psychology of Money', Morgan Housel says, 'Your personal experiences make up maybe 0.00000001% of what's happened in the world but maybe 80% of how you think the world works.'[8] This explains how you can have the same data or see the same things as another person and arrive at a completely different interpretation.

So, if you can't draw on an objective, external truth, and everything depends on perspective, then to get a more nuanced and useful overview of the situation you need to bring more perspectives to the discussion. The role of the project manager in this situation is not to be the expert but to get the right people in the room and attempt to reconcile multiple perspectives. When stories and opinions define reality, you need different skills to operate effectively.

If different interpretations can come from the same information, this raises an issue with the standard project approach. How do we develop a plan when we can't agree on what the problem looks like, or even if there is a problem? How do we define 'scope' in this situation? This brings us to the importance of naming the problem.

The importance of naming

Rittel and Webber's ninth trait is that 'a wicked problem can be explained in numerous ways' and that 'the choice of explanation determines the nature of the problem's resolution'.

In other words, how you describe the situation defines the solution. When you 'name' the situation, you have already decided what the solution is. Take a moment to reflect on that: it is a really important concept. The solution doesn't come from analysis, just naming.

The 1992 Los Angeles riots offer an extreme illustration of a wicked problem. What was the cause? Was it police brutality? A lack of police presence on the streets? A lack of public decency in the affected neighbourhoods? Frustration with a seemingly biased court system? Centuries of systemic racism? Disenchanted youth?

Regardless of what you believe the answer to be, as soon as you name the situation, you bound the solution and define what you need to do. If you name the cause as 'a lack of police on the streets', then the solution obviously involves more police officers or infrastructure.

Try this exercise. Get a few people in a room, pick a complex topic (like world hunger, climate change or poverty) and ask them to write down the significance of the problem and the main source of the problem. Then have each person, without sharing their thoughts, write down how they would go about fixing it. There is no doubt the solution they put forward will be driven by how they named the problem. And for extra credit, see how the topic you chose fits against the full list of wickedness traits in Box A.

Sometimes naming does more than just bring forward a solution: it conditions your mindset and drives your expectations without you even realising it. I was involved in a large project where, despite a detailed contract, the supplier and customer had a very different idea of what the project was about. You would never see their naming of the project written down – I doubt they were even aware of their differing perspectives – but it was clearly reflected in the way they operated. The supplier believed their role was to design, build and deliver a technically superior vehicle. The client wanted the supplier to reduce their acquisition risk and operational cost. This subtle but significant difference in naming created divergent behaviours between the two organisations, which drove delays and cost overruns. Changing the supplier's naming from 'delivering the technically best outcome' to 'having the client accept the product' led to a dramatic shift in behaviours, faster delivery and significant cost savings.

Take a moment to think of instances when changing the naming of a situation would lead to a significantly different outcome.

Unknowable

In the military, special forces operate in the most complex and emergent theatres of conflict. An Australian Commando told me about one of his days 'at work'. His team was dropped in to investigate and destroy a drug lab in Afghanistan. They had been briefed, they had previous experience, but there was no way of knowing exactly what they would face when they entered the building.

Two soldiers entered and, while searching the facility, a booby trap exploded, knocking out both of them. When Trooper P came to, he saw his buddy lying nearby, severely injured. His training kicked in and he went to work – he grabbed his medical kit, stabilised his partner and called a medevac, all despite the clear and present danger he faced from further explosions. Twenty minutes later they were both airlifted to hospital. He saved his mate and they both got to go home.

While your projects hopefully will never include the perils of a hot landing zone, some will surprise you no matter how much preparation you put in. Sometimes a situation will only reveal its true nature once you step into it; some things are unknowable in advance.

Not all projects are like this. Rolling out new desktop computers in a large organisation is relatively predictable and benign. If you do your research and prepare well, there should be very few surprises. So, how do we distinguish between those projects that are genuinely complex and those where the surprises are the result of a lack of preparation?

Fortunately, David Snowden's Cynefin framework provides a taxonomy to make sense of different situations. Originally published with C.F. Kurtz, the framework was developed to understand, among other things, situations where predictive models fail because there is no clear cause-and-effect relationship that can be identified and modelled.[9] The framework has evolved to identify five 'zones', as shown in Figure 2.2.[10]

Figure 2.2: The Cynefin framework

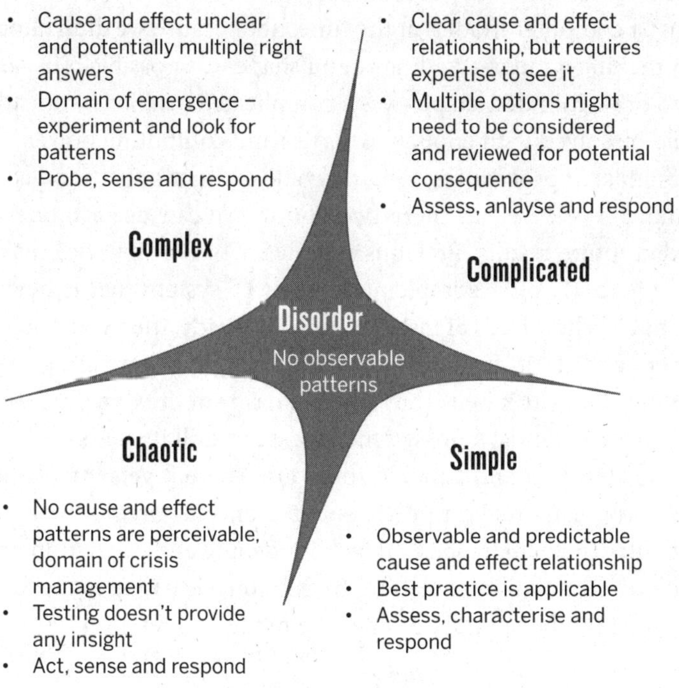

Complex or Complicated

The Cynefin framework makes a distinction between the zones on the right (Simple and Complicated) and those on the left (Complex and Chaotic). Kurtz and Snowden describe the left side as 'Un-order', where modelling based on experience doesn't work but patterns are still recognisable. I'm going to ignore Disorder because it is a very small space, has no discernible patterns and is beyond the scope of this discussion.

Simple and Complicated have observable and predictable cause-and-effect relationships. Compared to the Simple zone, Complicated requires more technical expertise, but both areas deal with topics that are known or knowable with enough research.

The Lockheed F-117 Nighthawk was the world's first operational stealth military jet designed to avoid radar detection. It is distinctive in the way its design has lots of straight edges, whereas later stealth aircraft are rounded. This was because of the limitations of computer models at the time, not because we didn't know that making a radar-avoiding round shape was possible. The ability to draw rounded shapes was a complicated problem – one that could be solved with enough expertise and computing power.

Standard procedures, analysis and reductionist modes of thinking work well in these two zones. We can use a model to predict future results. Previous experience or best practice makes sense here. If you are implementing an IT system that is new to you but has hundreds of installations worldwide, then you can hire someone to do it. It might be complicated, but there are proven methods that work well. The right-hand side of the Cynefin model is where the standard project management toolkit works.

The Complex and Chaotic zones are where it gets interesting, where you can't rely on previous experience to predict with any certainty what will happen. In fact, modelling and prediction provide no additional information. In this zone, learning is the focus and 'sense and respond' becomes the mode of operation.

The Complex zone is where experimentation and looking for patterns provide more insight than relying on previous examples or models. 'Action Learning' techniques work well in this zone. Prototypes aren't used to prove something has met the requirements so much as actually to define the requirements and rework the approach.

In the Chaotic zone, you can't predict, and you also can't rely on testing. The Ford Motor Company did extensive market research that showed a high level of demand for its new car brand launched in 1957; however, the Edsel was such a commercial disaster that it was removed from their line-up two years later. Elections are another example from the Chaotic zone: you can poll people before an election, but there is no guarantee they will vote that way on the day. Likewise, in large change programs in organisations, you may seek assurances from staff that they will support a program, but when it is implemented they might find a reason to disagree with it. There is no certainty. The reasons for what actually occurs are visible only in hindsight. This is a world of surprises and can leave you with the feeling of being let down when things don't go as expected. But this zone is not completely bad – it can also create a lot of energy, like we see at sporting events (see Box B, overleaf).

Complex projects, which cover both the Complex and Chaotic zones in the Cynefin framework, are characterised by these unknowables – questions that can be answered only by stepping into the situation. Complicated projects can be full of unknowns, but these can be resolved ahead of time if you do the work.

It is also important to keep in mind that many projects don't conform to a single classification. In Chapter 1, I mentioned the Empire State Building and what a huge success it was from a construction standpoint. It was a shining light of efficient project management. However, it was finished just as the Great Depression started and it would be 15 years before it was fully tenanted. Constructing the building might have been Complicated, but making money on it was Chaotic.

B: Sports are Chaotic

'Chaotic' isn't always bad. One of the things we like about sporting events is that they fall into the Chaotic zone. Sports have rules, but you can't predict the outcome with certainty. The result is affected by the state of the pitch, the weather, the condition of the ball, the mood of the players and the crowd, and even the choices of the referee.

Previous performance doesn't guarantee a particular outcome. The only way to know the result with certainty is to live through it.

No matter how much data you compiled, there was no way you could have predicted with certainty the combined sports results of 2016, a year in which:

- Leicester City won the English Premier League for the first time, starting the season at 5000-to-1 odds of taking the title
- the Chicago Cubs won the Major League Baseball World Series for the first time since 1908
- the Cronulla-Sutherland Sharks won their first National Rugby League title after 50 years in the competition.

The absence of certainty

So, in complex projects, you can't rely on prediction and there is no certainty. The answer, or even the problem, only reveals itself over time. If you find things are obvious only in hindsight, then it is probably a complex situation.

A large transformation I worked on involved significant consultation with unions. For reasons beyond the scope of the program, and only visible in hindsight, one union decided to drag the process out for as long as possible. What we hoped would be six meetings turned into more than a dozen. Some interactions planned for two hours went all day. Discussing the process with local delegates prior to the meetings didn't improve things. More analysis of the situation didn't help. It wasn't until we were in the consultation meetings that we would find out how they would go. You can imagine how this drove the project manager crazy due to having to rework the plan after each meeting.

Some might say everything is predictable with enough time and computing power, but these are intractable problems with significant unknowables where the only practical way to find out what will happen is to experience it. Your model will never be good enough (as discussed in Chapter 4), so live the experience and respond to what happens.

The overall purpose – along with belief in that purpose and ownership of the outcome – becomes the force that keeps you moving forward when there is a lack of certainty. The soldiers who entered the drug lab in Afghanistan put themselves in harm's way because they believed they served a higher purpose. You have to be okay with not knowing, believe in what you are doing and trust those around you. You have to learn to step into the future, then sense and respond to what happens.

Unique

My favourite pastime is to go sailing. I've been lucky enough to sail on many boats in different parts of the world, and every experience is different. Even though the physics of sailing is the same, there are stark differences that mean every boat is unique. Each crew has their own language and procedures, different calls can be made for each manoeuvre and they can prefer rum or beer. You need to learn what terms are used for different parts of the boat – a spinnaker 'brace' in one country is called a 'guy' somewhere else. There can even be fundamental differences in basic navigation. Most places in the world have their channel markers set up with green on the right (starboard) when entering a port, but North America has it around the other way, what they call 'red right returning'. So, what might seem like a standard activity requires an understanding of the specific situation.

The reality is similar for a complex project. While there might be comparable experiences to draw upon, it is the first time this problem is being addressed by this team in this environment.

The problem is unique

While the project might look similar to others, if it is complex it will be unique. The infrastructure project might use a design that is technically similar to a previous project, but it is dealing with a new group of interested parties with subtle but significantly different requirements and ways of working. The integrated software platform might be the same product as implemented elsewhere, but the state of the data or the willingness of the staff to accept new ways of working will be unique to this situation. The desire to say the project is the same as what has gone before – to link it to previous experience and pre-existing knowledge – is very strong, particularly in technical domains.

I love the insightful absurdity of Gary Larson's *The Far Side* cartoons. There is one where police discover someone in their apartment being swallowed by an alligator which is wrapped up by a snake. Despite the extraordinary situation, the detective says, 'I've seen this sort of thing before, Baxter… and it's *not* a pretty sight.'[11] This perfectly illustrates our desire to be the expert, to be in control even in unusual situations. How often do you see a project manager in a complex project demonstrate this attitude? No matter how unheard-of the situation is, they have been here before and they have it completely under control! They are unwilling to admit the situation is beyond their experience.

This is tied to the right-wrong paradigm of the technician, whereby everything has an answer and knowing the right answer is how you demonstrate value. At an individual level this can be linked to a sense of self-worth; or the desire to keep a job, pay the mortgage and provide for the family; or even to recapture past glories. When you consider the problem to be the same as one that has gone before, you will adopt previous ways of working, which can get in the way of being effective in this specific situation. Bring your experience, but open your mind to learning and creating something new. As Rittel and Webber's seventh trait has it: 'Every wicked problem is unique.'

The team is unique

In complexity, this group of people has not come together to solve this problem before. Therefore, a high priority in complex projects is to develop tools and techniques that work for the team to ensure effective interactions and guarantee the context is managed. New approaches, new relationships, new knowledge and new framing need to be established. This can be thrown out of kilter if your team grows too quickly. If rapid scale-up is required, then techniques need to be put in place to establish relationships and norms for how to operate in the emergent situation.

As a leader, you need to take the time to know the people you are dealing with and understand what they bring – to connect their minds, experience and expertise. Rather than hiding behind project processes such as status reports and governance meetings, take the time to set up relationships and ways of operating.

The environment is unique

If you hang around programs and portfolio management long enough, then someone will propose the implementation of standard templates and processes for managing the program. But blindly applying what has worked before can get in the way when it comes to complex projects.

John Seely Brown, former Chief Scientist at Xerox, suggests effective processes are highly dependent on the mindset of the organisation.[12] In complexity, the management processes have to make sense for the particular environment, the team's language and the nature of the problem they are working on. A project approval process that delivers all the required information in one organisation could be considered too complicated and bureaucratic in another. The ways of working have to evolve and match the situation. Capability and knowledge are generated by the way this particular group within this organisation operates and are codified in the processes they establish.

If you apply previous frameworks without regard for the situation, they will be ineffective. You need to take the time to understand the situation and its nuances – but time is something most projects are short on, so the leader is required to create space for this to occur. The need make time when everything is urgent is one of the core dilemmas of complex projects.

Constrained

All projects have constraints. Within complex projects the constraints – political, financial, legal – can be significant, creating high pressure, downside risk and heightened emotions. It often results in reduced degrees of freedom in decision-making, which can show up as more onerous and frequent reporting. This pressure, in turn, can impact your ability to think clearly and dispassionately, leading to ineffective reactions either in the design of the program or in response to issues. Yet constraints can also create focus and foster innovative outcomes.[13]

Many constraints aren't real

If you want to get to Mars from Earth using as little energy as possible, your best approach is to use a Hohmann transfer orbit, which requires you to use a specific launch window that opens up every 26 months. This is a real constraint dictated by gravity and the alignment of the planets.

Most constraints on complex projects, however, are social constructs. They occur because of the context of the project – limited funding in the organisation, political pressure to complete before the next election, management commitments to shareholders. They feel real but, unlike planetary motion, they are about human choices and can be questioned. They can also be misinterpreted.

I have seen projects take reasonable constraints and grow them into virtual molasses that gums up all interactions and slows down the project.

An airline maintenance project was struggling to meet its targets without the addition of expensive equipment to speed up engine changes. Despite a longstanding belief that project funding was limited, the team was encouraged to submit a request with a strong financial justification. To their amazement, the multi-million-dollar additional budget was approved and they succeeded in delivering a step change in aircraft availability because they questioned the constraints.

This is similar to another example in which a private company building infrastructure for a government agency was hampered by the approval process it encountered for any changes. Everyone believed the process was required to run the way it always had. When you pulled it apart, though, there were some probity rules to follow, but nothing that mandated the onerous and bureaucratic method that was used. The project team redesigned the process to include a detailed walk-through of any proposal, with teams free to discuss and debate issues in the request. This was followed by a formal submission with the expectation of rapid turnaround. This turned a process that would regularly take months into one completed in weeks, sometimes days, while still adhering to all the integrity obligations.

In complexity, it is essential to be able to identify the constraints and recognise which are real. An environment of high risk and low trust (driven by low certainty) can generate onerous restrictions that add to the complexity.

Constraints require us to be creative. The approach you choose should drive towards the project outcome while allowing for the real constraints, not those that are self imposed. Particularly when the project is under pressure, it is worth reflecting on which constraints can be questioned. Consider how many projects you have with constraints that everyone assumes are real when, in fact, they can be examined and changed, particularly around review and sign-off requirements. In complex projects, if you understand the reality of the constraints, you can redesign the approach to achieve significant shifts in performance. But if you are travelling to Mars, you are going to need to hit the right timing window.

The complexity characteristics summarised in Table 2.1 provide an insight into how complex projects differ from normal projects. You can probably see how the normal project management practices will break down in the face of these features.

Table 2.1: Complexity characteristics

Characteristic	Summary	Implications
Lots of **connected** parts	No single person can see the whole system	• Actions impact in unforeseen or unexpected ways. • Boundaries are difficult to define. • It's hard to divide the problem up into discrete parts. • If you can't know everything, then you have to rely on others for content and context.
Reality is **subjective**	Same information, different interpretations	• Multiple perspectives are working in the system. • More analysis doesn't provide better answers. • World views are significant – change the view, change the situation. • When you name the situation, you define the solution.

Characteristic	Summary	Implications
Some things are **unknowable**	This situation doesn't reveal itself until you step into it	• The situation is emergent (it keeps changing with new information) and our understanding is unstable. • Planning in more detail doesn't help. • It is not due to lack of upfront research – understanding only comes from action. • 'Not knowing' creates discomfort.
Unique situation	First time this group has solved this problem in this situation	• You need to build new knowledge, relationships and framing. • Some parts are familiar, but it is the first time for this whole setup. • You can't rely on 'best practice'.
Significantly **constrained**	Constraints are amplified by high visibility and impact	• Many constraints aren't real, but rather extrapolated from more basic concerns. • Downside risk heightens emotions, creating pressure, which drives ineffective responses. • Design the approach to address the constraints.

Working with complexity

Beyond the individual characteristics that drive the complexity level of the project, there are also two overall features of complex projects that are worth noting: that the level of complexity is always changing, and complex projects can have a significant impact on business performance.

Complexity isn't constant

The level of complexity changes over the course of a project, and your techniques need to adjust as this occurs. In general, it drops through the life of the project as questions are answered, decisions are made and teams develop ways to work together. However, complexity can increase as new questions arise, issues are ignored and divisions grow. It increases if stakeholders aren't kept in the loop and they demand more and more input into decisions, adding their perspectives to the mix; and it increases when milestones are missed and greater constraints are put on the way the project operates. Some projects hold their level of complexity to the end, like negotiations where decisions are held until the last moment with an 'all or nothing' result.

Also, as already mentioned, there is no pure model of complexity. It is common to find that parts of a project can be simple or complicated while others remain complex and chaotic. Every project will have a different profile. The first step is to understand the level and nature of the complexity in your projects.

Complex projects are worth doing well

Technically complicated projects, with their need for rare specialist skills, used to be the most valuable and hardest projects to deliver. But the proliferation of consultants with codified knowledge, and the ready exchange of information, has made it easier to buy that expertise in the market. These days, the most valuable projects – innovation, business transformation, new business models and large, one-off developments – have all the characteristics of complexity. Complex projects have high leverage. They can underpin your business success but also see it lose ground dramatically if they fail to deliver. They are unique and difficult to replicate, and are a source of advantage if done well.

As I mentioned at the beginning of the chapter, there is a range of complexity models and assessment tools covering dozens of different factors that dissect what it means for a project to be complex. The majority of these factors can be described by the five characteristics identified in this chapter. For example, some models define how complexity rises with the number of disciplines required, the interdependency of benefits and the range of stakeholders involved, which can all be explained by the fact that the situation is connected and subjective.

These five characteristics of complexity force us to question the assumptions that standard project management relies on – in particular, the idea that you can know what you need to do ahead of time, or at least very quickly find out. The standard approach is not designed for the types of problems that are connected, subjective and full of unknowns. Standard project management works for simple and complicated projects, but when facing the ambiguity inherent in complex projects it is incomplete.

Chapter 3
AN INCOMPLETE TOOLKIT

'It ain't what you don't know that gets you into trouble. It's what you know for sure that just ain't so.'
—Anonymous

The challenge with complex projects is that the standard project management toolkit is more at home coordinating resources on known problems. In its traditional form it is a system that was created in an industrial context for the purpose of delivering large-scale efficiency. While it has evolved over time, the underlying push for predictability and control makes it harder to deal with the emergence and unknowns inherent in complexity.

Symptoms of complexity can appear to be addressed by improved project process, but any problems will persist until the underlying social wickedness is addressed. Standard project practice delivers an improvement, but without addressing the root causes of the complexity, the improvement is only short-term.

These gaps in the standard project toolkit, where insufficient energy is focused on the characteristics of complexity, have left competent project managers unprepared and struggling to be effective. This is because their mode of thinking and toolkit drive ineffective reactions which might create initial results but make matters worse when problems arise.

The standard toolkit comes up short

When I talk about the standard project toolkit, I'm referring to the common methods and mindsets you can find in most project management books or courses. It represents a standard way to manage projects – from initiation, to planning, to execution and close-out – that is prescriptive and process-based. It actively looks to remove any surprises, ideally before the project starts, through tight scope definition and a robust plan. Resources are allocated and uncertainty is handled using a process to identify and mitigate risks. There is regular tracking to ensure everything is progressing as expected. Any variation is addressed and brought back into line or explained, justified and replanned in detail.

The unwavering focus is on keeping everything under control. At any point in time, you have the knowledge and confidence to prove when the project will deliver.

All of this is based on the mindsets, introduced in Chapter 1, that pervade the standard project approach, such as focusing on what needs to be delivered, relying on documentation and planning, and reducing uncertainty through tight process control.

These mindsets influence how you interpret the situation, guide decision-making and affect how you react to issues.

However, what initially appear to be good project practices, which have been successful in many normal projects, can lead you to take actions that are ineffective in complexity. The usual approach, with its desire to reduce ambiguity, will drive you to 'name and tame' the problem as quickly as possible in order to scope and bound the problem. However, this is unproductive when the topic is connected, subjective and still emerging. How can you rely on the contract documentation when many of the real conundrums were unknowable when it was written? Overall, the mindsets of the standard project management toolkit are at odds with the characteristics of complexity.

The impact of the mismatch will propagate over time. It won't be obvious at first, but then frustration will grow as you start to run into some predictable symptoms:

- Plans continue to slip despite the best efforts of everyone on the project.
- Significant surprises occur despite risk management forums.
- Key decisions get revisited, causing delay and annoyance.
- People lose confidence that the project is under control.

The fundamental problem is that the management approach is based on a paradigm that doesn't match the situation. It's like having a screw that you need to drive into a block of wood, but you only have hammers. So, you get a hammer and start hitting the screw, but it's not going in, so you get a bigger hammer, with much the same result. Eventually you get a hammer big enough to force the screw in until it sits flush with the wood. It might look like the result you wanted, but it's not going to hold; it's not going to give you the outcome you were aiming for. It has taken a lot of effort and made a big mess. That's what we see happening here: more and more effort being applied so the project will look like it's finished.

And here is the real sting in the tail. If the standard toolkit failed the project to begin with because of the mismatch to complexity, the common reactions – which seem normal and reasonable and are designed to bring it back on track – have the opposite effect of what was intended, creating a vicious cycle and accelerating the project towards failure.

Logical reactions make things worse

You may have experienced a situation on a project that is in trouble in which the frequency of steering committee meetings increases from monthly to fortnightly in order to exert more control. This increased frequency, and the underlying nature of the project's complexity, generate more questions, requiring more work by team members to gather information and more time to present it to the committee. Now the meetings are extended from one hour to two hours to cope with the increased content.

The project support team becomes overwhelmed with data requests and annoyed because nothing has been fixed – in their eyes, the situation just got worse. They are producing more and more information with less time to distil it into something meaningful. They are frustrated because they see nothing improving when, at least to them, the answer seems obvious and these meetings aren't getting to the heart of the matter.

Senior executives start to worry that the project has lost its way. Overwhelmed by the barrage of additional information, they start to lose confidence that the project team knows what it is doing. They feel they can no longer trust the answers they're getting because more detail doesn't provide insights, only more questions.

This insidious downward spiral in an example of how action that appears to be a sensible response to a problem creates more issues than it resolves.

Most people would agree that when a project is in trouble, there are standard responses that work to bring it back on track: focus on delivery, improve the plan, get into the detail, go back to the original documentation to confirm the scope and, in extreme cases, change the team. While they will work for a well-defined project, in a complex situation they exacerbate the problems and hasten its demise. They are a common and repeated series of ineffective reactions to a project in distress and highlight the need for a different way of thinking.

Reaction 1: Focus on delivering something

Make decisions and take action – that's the mantra for this reaction. The logic goes that by getting 'runs on the board' you show something for your effort and build capability for completion; you build a delivery mindset by actually delivering something. 'We all know what we need to do – we just have to get on with it' (see Box C, over the page). When the path forward is clear, this might be a great strategy; but when you are dealing with complexity, where things are emergent and connected, it ignores wider implications.

It is often easy to give the impression of progress – the legendary 'quick win' – without addressing the real issues affecting the project. This creates an immediate sense of achievement but locks in a more significant negative impact on the long-term value of the project. The single-minded focus on delivery for its own sake is fundamentally flawed: it constrains the future, reduces ambition and can let other issues in the project run out of control, and still not address the complexity at the heart of the problem.

Delivering now constrains the future

The rush to make decisions means that choices are based on what information is available now, setting judgements in concrete and moving on. Early decisions have high leverage on a project and are expensive to change later. In complexity, the cause and effect of decisions are separated over time and the result of the decisions might not show up for months. When the implications of decisions become apparent, and with the weight of new information (and no doubt questions from outside the project), the team face a choice: press on with the choices made, living with the suboptimal outcome, or revisit the decision and cope with all the resulting angst, effort and cost.

This common reaction was used on a project to deliver a new military aircraft. On the back of production delays and customisation of components, the complexity started to rise.

C: 'We all know what we need to do – we just have to get on and do it.'

I'd been sitting in the review session for almost three hours. This infrastructure design project was in deep trouble. Deadlines had been slipping since the project started. Design sign-off was only a few months away and there was a high probability that this deadline, like all those before it, would be missed. Any further delay would increase public scrutiny on the infrastructure operator. The delays had destroyed the project's profitability, and with launch dates slipping there was increasing pressure to get it done. This review session had been called to get all the issues out on the table so the project could be brought back on track.

During the discussion, a range of issues was raised and debated, such as problems with the design review process, the budget overrun on engineering design work and the difficulty with some suppliers running behind on their deliverables. It was clear that the issues were complex and connected, with lots of tentacles reaching into different parts of the organisation and out to external suppliers.

The meeting had already run an hour over the original two-hour time limit and, with no simple remedy emerging, the program manager said we were making it all too complex. 'The plan is very clear. We all know what we need to do – we just need to get on and do it.' And with that declaration, to the relief of many in the room, the meeting ended.

The instruction was based on the misguided belief that everyone had the same view of 'what we need to do'. Over the coming weeks, nothing changed. The project continued to diverge from the plan and lurch towards financial disaster.

How often do you see that simply 'sticking to the plan' ignores the real complexity of the situation? This approach assumes that the plan properly represents all the intricacies and connections and issues. The reality is that plans don't describe the connectedness and depth of intervention required. The team needs a way to lay out what they are facing, develop a common understanding and provide feedback from their particular perspective before you can claim that 'we all know what to do'.

Delays crept into the project, much to the chagrin and frustration of the customer. The response from the program manager was to focus on the next major milestone: the sign-off of the aircraft by the local air safety regulators. The team focused on achieving sign-off as soon as possible. When this was accomplished, it gave them confidence they were getting the project back on track.

But this was just the beginning of their problems; this apparent win guaranteed much greater issues for the project. The certification of the aircraft specified a baseline configuration that was defined as 'airworthy', and any change to the baseline had to be documented and confirmed. This constrained the ability to freely change or update components on the aircraft as development progressed. The longer process of certification caused further delays to the project.

As the delays grew, the focus turned to the contract, and the whole thing ended up in court. Unfortunately, the contract hadn't considered the specific situation that had arisen – the certification of the aircraft while changes were still being made. What was supposed to be a low-risk project grew into a contractual mess.

The singular focus on applying normal project management techniques had missed the wider implications, and the assumption that the contract could resolve the issues was also misguided. The reality was that the drive to hit the defined milestones compromised the delivery of the whole program.

Rushing to tame a complex situation and deliver without understanding all the connections and implications locks in a path that constrains the future. Often the real implications won't be known until much later, when it is either too late or extremely expensive to make a change.

Focus on delivery reduces ambition

An undeviating focus on delivery drives you to reduce risk and uncertainty and produce something that is within the direct control of the team. This means anything creative or ambitious is removed in preference of something that can be guaranteed.

In the worst cases it becomes a face-saving exercise: what is the minimum we can get done to show something was delivered? I've seen projects stop all change requests or cut large segments out of the program scope to be able to show progress. The underlying mindset is to reduce the scope to something achievable, but never mention the loss of value.

Believing in silver bullets amplifies issues

A more extreme version of the 'deliver something' mentality is the belief that pulling a single large lever will turn the whole situation around. This is what I call 'silver-bullet thinking' – the belief that a single magical solution will solve the entire problem. In the NFL it's called the 'Hail Mary pass' – the one desperate shot at glory.

A new CEO in a transport company faced a major contract that was in trouble. He spent time understanding the problem, then focused on one solution: a new program manager. He addressed any significant issues only when they became critical, because all his attention was on the selection of the new manager. By the time the new person came on board, a few months had passed, and the program had deteriorated and was almost unrecoverable. This silver-bullet approach ignored the connectedness of complex situations. It was a simplistic tactic that, in trying to deal with one issue in isolation, allowed the rest of the project to unravel.

Clearly, then, it is not just about delivering something. That focuses too much on the short term. The next reaction is to take a wider view and build a better plan.

Reaction 2: Improve the plan

Any project manager worth their salt will tell you that the most crucial thing in a project is a decent plan. A good plan is the path to success – it coordinates and prioritises effort, and can be shared and tracked. To quote a project manager I worked with, 'We just need a more detailed plan so everyone knows what they need to do.' In a command-and-control, centrally planned system the centre can tell everyone what to do. In detail. And then track it.

The problem with this is that, to adjust a military phrase, no plan survives first contact with reality. At the heart of complexity is 'wickedness', meaning every action you take changes the situation, which in turn requires the plan to be adjusted. And the normal process of baselining the plan and checking progress against that baseline guarantees the status report will rush into the red (unless team members hide that fact until reality overwhelms the reporting, but that's a different issue altogether). The plan was never real in the first place because of the level of unknowns (see Box D, overleaf).

A plan is useful, but blindly going into detailed planning in complexity is a recipe for creating significant rework in an unstable system. It leads to the feeling of always being behind and wasting energy updating a plan that is already out of date. The team will end up feeling they spend more time adjusting the plan than getting work done. And the more time they spend updating and monitoring the detail, the greater the chance they will miss issues of significance.

In complexity, you are standing on shifting sands. The more you plan, the more it becomes obvious that the plan doesn't properly describe the changing situation. But maybe you are just missing some of the details.

Reaction 3: Get more detail

When things continue to change and simple answers can't be provided, the normal reaction is to go into more detail. Blame is placed on an incomplete understanding of the situation. So, more detail should provide greater clarity, understanding and trust – but in complexity it does the opposite.

Detail doesn't generate insight

In *Blink*, Malcolm Gladwell describes military and medical situations where despite an array of available information, 'you need to know very little to find the underlying signature of a

D: The re-baseline dilemma

See if any of this sounds familiar. A significant project is set up to transform part of your business. A plan is put in place and 'baselined'. The baseline takes a snapshot of the timing and estimated effort, which allows any variation to be identified, tracked and remediated.

Everything goes well for a few months, but then changes occur. Maybe new information comes to light about the extent of change resistance encountered, or you are asked to slow the project down because of the potential frontline impact on sensitive negotiations that are underway about a new pay deal. Whatever the cause, the result is that the plan no longer matches reality. The status report is now covered in red ink.

Now what? You have two choices: you can carry on reporting progress against the original plan or you can 're-baseline' the plan, resetting all the targets based on the new information.

If you keep the plan as it is, you continue to honour the original commitments and hold the team to account for what they promised. However, the report will always be red and you will lose visibility of any progress or improvements. Everyone knows the timeline is not achievable and the ongoing red status demotivates the team. It also lacks integrity because the plan doesn't genuinely reflect your understanding of the situation.

If you update the plan, you acknowledge that the original plan was overambitious and fundamentally flawed. But in doing this, are you letting the project manager off the hook and not holding them to account for what was originally agreed? What does it mean to have a plan if no one is held to account for it? What if the situation isn't stable enough to actually produce a new plan that can be relied on? These questions are ignored in standard project management approaches, which are built on the belief that the future can be predicted and planned.

Re-baselining the project is the most common reaction and makes a lot of practical sense, but it can come with recriminations from those who believe in the sanctity of the plan: Why didn't you know? What could you have done to build a better plan? How can we believe in the new plan? All of this leads to the question: what is the role of the plan in a complex project when it can't precisely predict the future?

complex phenomenon'.[1] In fact, the availability of more information led to poorer decisions because it confused and slowed the decision-making process.

The heavily intertwined nature of complexity, in which multiple individual perspectives are important, means more information creates more questions. These drag you further into detail or down blind alleys, making it harder to see what is significant which, in turn, creates more arguments about which perspective is correct.

For example, the 'simple' question of how many people are affected by a change might lead you to look at what rosters are in place for the frontline staff. In doing this you realise that the rosters have been heavily customised, so you need to understand the situation at a crew level to get a solid answer. In doing this you find that crews are made up of different groups, each with their own characteristics, some dating back decades. With every step down in detail you are moving further away from the top-line answer and further into uncertainty.

More detail does not provide clarity, either because of the large number of unknowns or because of the connected nature of complexity; it just generates more lines of inquiry. It creates extra work for no significant gain. This reaction to 'get more detail' is based on the assumption that unknowns exist because you haven't done enough work and that more detail will provide better answers. It is the fundamental mistake of applying a reductionist mindset to a problem that requires synthesis and insight. It is like trying to understand why you like the Queen song 'Bohemian Rhapsody' by reading academic papers about lyrics and melodies. Detail creates the appearance of understanding while breeding confusion.

Vortex of distrust

Has anyone ever said to you, 'It can't be this hard; just give me an answer'? As you dig down into more detail you see the connectedness of the system, but with insufficient time for contemplation you lose the ability to see the whole system.

The vortex of distrust looks like this: Manager asks for a quick answer. Analyst gets the data at a high level, but it contains some imprecision and uncertainty (because of the emergent nature of the situation). Manager asks for it to be 'right'. Analyst digs into detail, finds more data, generates a slightly different answer. Manager questions why things changed and asks for more proof and documentation of the situation. Analyst writes it out, but in doing so creates more questions (because of the nuances of language) and potentially a different answer. Manager is now frustrated by Analyst's inability to document precisely and asks why the numbers keep changing. Any further request from Manager will require more detail in order to trust the numbers and the Analyst.

The dive into detail hits the project team particularly hard. People work long hours to prepare the detail… and then it changes, again. Team members don't know if they are doing the right thing, because the goalposts keep being moved.

If the detail is available, it creates confusion; if it isn't available, it creates frustration. Both of these responses drive a vicious cycle of more detail, less clarity and growing distrust. But if you can't trust the people, then hopefully you can trust the documentation!

Reaction 4: Trust the documentation

When the detail doesn't help you to understand the situation because it keeps changing, the next reaction is to go back to the original documentation – the scope document or contract – to create certainty. Documents don't suffer the vagaries of opinions, and besides, everyone agreed to it upfront. However, given the emergent nature of the complex projects, often the original document is incomplete or based on flawed assumptions.

There are plenty of examples of the world changing during the project: the technology project that was set up to implement a new system but the supplier was taken over by a competitor, or the infrastructure development that had financing arrangements put together just before the Global Financial Crisis and needed everything to go just right to be financially viable. I can guarantee that the original documentation for these projects no longer reflected what was going on or made sense in the altered context they found themselves in.

Standing firm with the documentation might make sense in a simple or even complicated project, in which you can draw on experience and the plan doesn't change dramatically because most issues have been predicted. But complex projects change as new understanding emerges. Relying on documentation written months or even years ago, when everyone was enthusiastic and full of confidence, can be a fundamentally flawed approach.

A contract is an attempt to create an external truth – one that doesn't depend on opinions and perspectives. Most contracts are written in case the relationship no longer works. Most projects, particularly complex ones, stand on the hope that things will go well. The contract tells you how to play when things are falling apart. If you are using it to manage the project relationships from day to day, you are on a path to big problems, if you don't have them already. Trusting the contract to provide the complete answer in complexity might sort out some of the money, but it definitely won't fix the timeline, and it reduces the chance of delivering the outcome.

Reaction 5: Change the team and reset the project

The final reaction is simple and common. When all else fails, replace the project manager and reset the project. Sometimes this is necessary, but it rarely addresses the heart of the matter. In fact, it increases the complexity – a new team means new ways of operating to be established – and sends you back to the beginning again. This reaction will fail if the next person brings the same standard project management mindset and approach and is not prepared to address the nature of the complexity that led the previous manager or team to fail.

In complex projects, all of these reactions appear to create progress. However, this is a dangerous illusion of improvement because they never really address the core issue – in the long run, they ignore and amplify it. They create predictable breakdowns, because they constitute an incomplete approach that does not address the heart of the problem.

Reactions don't address the heart of complexity

These ineffective reactions represent an inability or unwillingness to deal with – or even notice – the underlying wickedness of the situation.

It's like the problem of claypans faced by many farmers. A claypan is a layer of clay just below the surface of a field. This layer prevents the movement of water and nutrients, which dramatically reduces the productivity of the area. All the work and expense put into the normal activities of tilling and fertilising will help the plants get established, and it looks like progress is being made as the plants start to grow, but the field will never live up to its full potential until the clay is broken up and water can move freely. It might look like something is happening, but there won't be a real breakthrough until you address the underlying problem: the claypan itself.

Complex projects can be like this field, with the claypan being the dark heart of wickedness sitting below the surface that represents opinions not expressed, agendas not surfaced and concerns not raised. Most people know it's there but figure (or hope) the project can be delivered without having to address it.

When the complexity can no longer be ignored, the first attempt to improve things may be to add a process to help manage the relationship – perhaps a new status report or a revised meeting agenda. It addresses some of the concerns but avoids the core issue, just as fertiliser improves the soil but does nothing about the water flow.

Table 3.1: Summary of reactions

Reaction		
1 Just deliver something	Underlying logic	**Focus on what needs to be delivered:** quick wins show what it takes to get something done.
	What gets in the way	Inability to see the whole picture and being thwarted by things you don't know.
	What happens	Lock in choices that constrain the future, reduce ambition to something simple and potentially amplify issues.
2 Improve the plan	Underlying logic	**Control the process to remove uncertainty:** a decent plan is the path to success. It coordinates and prioritises effort, and is used to focus and control effort.
	What gets in the way	Too many unknowns make the plan unstable, requiring constant rework; the plan updates can't keep up with the changing situation.
	What happens	Plan doesn't reflect reality, leading to an increase in planning effort and distracting the team from identifying real issues.
3 Get more detail	Underlying logic	**More detail provides greater understanding:** everything is understandable with enough effort or expertise.
	What gets in the way	It's heavily intertwined – more connections and opinions show up as you go into detail.
	What happens	Detail doesn't create insight but rather confusion and a vortex of distrust, which leads to increased workload.
4 Trust the documentation	Underlying logic	**Original documentation is critical:** it is the one thing that's stable and not open to opinions; effort was put in up-front to get it right and everyone agreed to it.
	What gets in the way	It was written without full information and no longer matches the situation.
	What happens	Results in compromises in what gets delivered and distracts the team from delivering the project.
5 Change the team	Underlying logic	**Find an expert:** the problem is a lack of ability to cope with the situation.
	What gets in the way	Takes time to replace team members, and if the new team brings the same toolkit, it doesn't fix the issue.
	What happens	Go back to square one.

As the project progresses and things continue to struggle, another crutch is added – maybe more detailed reporting or daily updates – but the wickedness remains. This slicing of the problem to deal with issues one at a time avoids, and even tries to mask, the underlying complexity. For example, the focus on 'just delivering something' turns everyone's minds to building things and leaves little time to address the social interactions required to lift performance and deliver the outcomes.

The project will deliver something but, like the underperforming field, it will never reach its potential without taking on a new way of operating.

So, what's missing?

The problem in complexity is not a failure to correctly apply the standard project process: it is that the standard process is rendered ineffective by the underlying characteristics of complexity. The standard toolkit is anchored in a model of management that is centred on predictability and control. This approach stands on the belief that the situation can be well defined, or at least bounded, ahead of time and then any variation can be managed.

When project managers rely on the usual assumptions about how projects operate, they make at least one of the following mistakes:

- **They remove ambiguity prematurely:** Defining scope, building a plan and creating boundaries that allow performance to be tracked are the first things on the agenda in the standard approach. When the situation is complex and many things are still unknown, this creates unreasonable expectations of clarity and certainty. It also guarantees the need for rework as information emerges and the plan gets changed.

- **They don't put enough focus on the bigger picture:** In complexity there is clarity at a high enough level. When problems occur, the tendency is to go down into the detail, which takes you away from clarity. The result is ineffective and even dysfunctional decision-making, because the manager and leaders are focused on the details and overwhelmed by the complexity, operating without a clear picture of what's important and where to focus effort.
- **They underestimate the importance of humanity:** Project managers can hide in the technical project process and use terms like 'managing stakeholders' rather than connecting with people as individuals. An unwillingness to engage with people and seek out opinions, with all the messiness and doubt that comes with that, ensures that disagreements fester and grow until they can no longer be ignored.

Status reports can be updated on time and presented in detail, but the downward slide continues when we replicate these common mistakes.

A new approach

I have seen experienced and successful program directors who delivered significant outcomes in other project environments struggle to get things done when the situation is complex. They have followed the standard processes diligently and done everything the manual says but have still fallen short. They have found themselves facing situations in which the universe no longer works the way they expect it to. And the more they have applied their trusted, mechanistic ways, the worse the situations have become. It is like throwing water on an oil fire – well-intentioned but misguided, because the situation is beyond their understanding and their reaction makes things much worse.

Unfortunately, the emergent nature of complex projects, when managed in a mechanistic way, breeds toxicity – difficult relations, frustrated and injured staff, long hours and frazzled minds. If you are operating in a challenging environment where the reactions that have worked before are failing you – where the team is looking for leadership and a way through the fog but the guidance from managers is 'projects are hard; get used to it' – it doesn't have to be this way. These projects require a different approach and an extended toolkit that is built for the situation.

You have to change the way you operate, to rethink the overall approach rather than making minor adjustments. You can't just reuse the old system. The world has changed. I'm not suggesting throwing out everything you know about project management, but rather, levelling up to an enhanced project toolkit – a set of mindsets, practices and skills that copes with complexity rather than trying to ignore it.

We need to spend more time connecting with people rather than analysing the plan. We need to be resilient and persistent, always looking for a way forward. And we have to become comfortable with ambiguity so that we do not try to tame the situation too quickly. I'm proposing that we need new capabilities we don't normally associate with project managers, like asking good questions, listening skills and storytelling.

Some will say, 'We don't need to change that much. We've already dealt with it. We're Agile and we've got new and different methods.' Agile, which is a form of iterative project management, is a very common approach today, but the problem – which will be covered in more detail in Chapter 5 – is that Agile and these other methods are focused mainly on the 'build' phase of a project. These methods are not designed to question whether we are solving the right problem in the first place.

The main barrier to success is resistance to operating in a different way and committing the time it will take to build the new toolkit. What I'm proposing here is an approach that's quite different from the way most project managers normally operate. It requires a willingness to abandon the illusion of control created by the standard project processes in favour of a different method that increases the likelihood of delivering real results.

Complex projects are different and valuable. If you want to succeed, you have to realise that the assumptions and ways of thinking inherent in the standard project management model don't work in complexity. If you want to excel at projects that are significant and distinctive, then you have to realise that when it comes to complex projects, we bought the wrong thinking model.

Chapter 4
WE BOUGHT THE WRONG THINKING MODEL

'You cannot solve a problem with the same thinking that created it.'
—Albert Einstein

So, it is clear that complex projects are different and pose significant challenges for the standard project toolkit. It is not enough just to think up alternative activities and hope everything will be fine, because the underlying desire for prediction and control remains. We need to strip back the analytical paradigm that guides all the actions and ways of working in the standard project model and find an alternative approach – one that shifts the emphasis from prediction to learning. What's required is a way of thinking that works with, rather than pushes against, the characteristics of complexity. Design thinking represents this alternative model and is a proven performer in complex situations.

The origin of project management is science

To understand the mental model that underpins the standard project management toolkit, we need to understand the rise of scientific thought and its influence on modern management practices.

Creating reliability – the rise of science

After being lost in the Middle Ages, what we recognise as modern scientific concepts started to reappear in the Western world during the Renaissance. Works were recovered from Ancient Greece and ideas preserved from the Islamic Golden Age. The result was the Scientific Revolution, which began in the 16th century and was a movement away from the vagaries of personal experience towards a trust in robust external observation.

René Descartes, one of the founders of modern philosophy, believed in mathematical thinking over flawed sensory experiences, and that true knowledge could be derived only from reason rather than personal observation. Diverging from philosophy, science's goal was objective understanding, removed from the tainted aspirations and biases of individuals. This thinking underpinned the Age of Enlightenment, which saw the explosion of different branches of scientific inquiry such as astronomy, botany, zoology, physics and chemistry.

Knowledge came from teasing things apart into their constituent elements in order to better understand them. More detail provided greater insight into the world and a better understanding of what was true. Evidence-based processes, with rigorous observation along with inductive and deductive methods, became the backbone of scientific inquiry. This allowed us to understand and harness the world, to analyse and predict how things would react.

This new approach to understanding and knowledge was encapsulated in the scientific approach, which I've distilled down to five themes (as shown in Table 4.1).

Table 4.1: Five themes of the scientific approach

Theme	Description
Descriptive	Science is about explaining the world as it exists today. It creates a model for prediction by deeply understanding what exists.
Empirical	Rigorous observations and consistent data are prioritised over the flawed aspirations and biases of individuals.
Provable	Any interpretation beyond what is observed is based on inductive or deductive logic.
Reductionist	More detail about the constituent parts creates a better understanding of the situation and the ability to master a domain. This drives scientists to create more and more focus and delineation between topics.
Replicable	The same experiment under the same conditions creates the same results. Any variables or conditions not being studied are standardised to provide confidence in the results.

The scientific approach fundamentally shifted how humans operated in the natural world. It made it possible for us to constantly evolve our understanding from generation to generation. Scientific models could reliably predict what would happen – the best conditions for growing crops, or the maximum load before a bridge would fail.

The growth in understanding of the natural world led to increasing freedom from drudgery and hard labour. This ensured that science, with its promise of power over nature and ongoing improvement, was the primary mode of thinking for centuries.

Science brought control into organisations

On the back of the Scientific Revolution came the Industrial Revolution, with larger and larger machines that outgrew domestic operations. These massive contraptions needed to be powered on an enormous scale, which led to the rise of factories and the organisations to operate them. Given the success of science in driving the industrial growth, it wasn't long before the scientific method was applied to managing these organisations.

In the early 20th century, scientific management was a predominant mode of thought, as it promised control over the ever-expanding organisations. In 1911 Frederick Winslow Taylor published *The Principles of Scientific Management*, which introduced a scientific approach to organisational management based on planning, measurement and feedback loops to drive the optimal use of resources and get the most from an operation.[1] Around the same time, Henri Fayol developed his management theories, referred to as Fayolism, which identified the five functions of management: planning, organising, staffing, directing and controlling.[2] Across the world, on assembly lines and construction projects, in mines and other forms of industry, efficiency and reliability were the focus.

Project management took on the same promise

At the same time, project management as a professional discipline was on the rise. While it had been around for centuries, project management was now being codified as a standard method. A colleague of Taylor's, Henry Gantt, along with others, looked to apply the same level of rigor to projects as in scientific management.

Project management practice has been built on the concepts of Fayolism: planning, organising, staffing, directing and controlling. The standardisation of the approach allows a common set of actions to be applied in a repeatable way. The focus on documentation (scope, charter, contract, plan) removes opinions and measures performance objectively.

Once you appreciate the scientific nature of project management, what becomes clear is how much faith we put in plans to predict the future and track performance against those predictions. That's what stands in the way of dealing with uncertainty and the emergence of complexity. The scientific model is alluring because it provides certainty wrapped up in simple, provable facts, but this model doesn't work for complexity.

The scientific approach is incompatible with complexity

As described in Chapter 2, complexity is created by individual perspectives and the unique situations that emerge around us. Complexity is all about humanity, but scientific approaches work to remove the individual from the situation, to eliminate the 'flawed' sensory experiences and aspirations of individuals and groups.

Additionally, the elements of a complex situation are connected, and when they are pulled apart into discrete boxes they lose their essence. The whole system is more than the sum of its parts. However, modern science is becoming more and more focused, specialised and reductionist, which means it no longer operates as an 'integrated realm' that looks at the whole system.[3]

Finally, science works to describe 'what is' based on what has gone before, but in complex projects we are not dealing with the repeat of a previous situation. We are trying to make sense of where we are now without directly modelling or extrapolating from the past. The scientific approach is incompatible with this.

The fundamental problem in complex projects, as shown in Table 4.2 overleaf, is that the themes of the scientific method are incompatible with the characteristics of complexity.

Other scientific methods try to cope with complexity but come up short

Before going any further, I want to take a moment to address formal scientific theories of complexity. A range of models have evolved to deal with feedback loops and other complicating factors – chaos theory for nonlinear dynamics, nondeterministic algorithms in computer science and complex adaptive systems with heterogeneous actors, to name a few.

But these notions run into problems. Nonlinear dynamics is good at explaining how balls move on a billiard table, but it breaks down if the balls have free will to move out of the way. Network theory is brilliant at modelling airline operations, until industrial disruptions create uncertainty about when an airport will operate. Most models struggle to deal effectively with the concept of emergence – the system having properties that none of its elements contain on their own, such as how life emerges from what is essentially a group of rudimentary atoms arranged into molecules, cells and systems.

Table 4.2: How the scientific approach is incompatible with complexity

Scientific theme	Description	Incompatibility with complexity characteristics
Descriptive	Focus on what is	Some things are unknowable beforehand, making it impossible to describe the situation in full. Emergence and creativity change what 'is' over time.
Empirical	Data based, not driven by the opinions of individuals	Reality is subjective and depends on which individuals are in the room – it is completely about opinions. Constraints are mostly socially derived.
Provable	Inductive or deductive logic	Some things are unknowable beforehand, with no predictable cause–effect relationship.
Reductionist	Understanding comes from detail	Many connected parts in the situation make it difficult to pull apart, and more detail only creates confusion.
Replicable	Conducting the same experiment will yield the same results	Each project is unique and will face different challenges and agendas.

Complex projects are intractable

Scientific complexity theories deal with Complicated problems rather than Complex and Chaotic situations, as described on the Cynefin map in Chapter 2. In complex projects, the boundaries of the system are not clear and the true nature of interactions is unknowable. This makes it extremely difficult to model and predict. Complex situations fall into the group of problems referred to as 'intractable' – they might be theoretically solvable but it's impractical to do so.

Predicting the outcome of a football match is an intractable problem. Despite the clear set of rules, the result is affected by a range of physical attributes (temperature, humidity, wind, light) and social interactions (mood of the players, influence of the crowd). Theoretically you could model the situation, but it would be more complex than the actual event.

It takes more time to model an intractable problem than to actually live it. If I ask an eight-year-old to build something using six of the original 2 × 4 LEGO blocks, there are more than 915 million possible outcomes.[4]

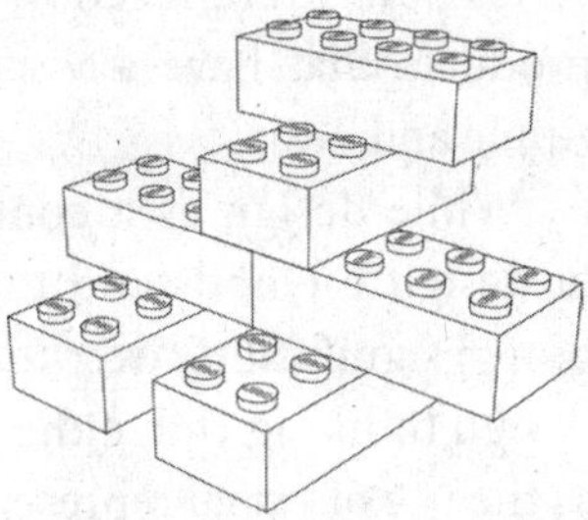

I can model all these potential outcomes, but how do I predict what the child will actually build? Or I can wait a few seconds to find out.

Sometimes it is faster and easier to live through the experience and respond to what happens than to try to predict it.

From prediction to understanding as the organising idea

Fundamentally, science is about creating predictive models that explain our world, but these models aren't designed to handle intractable problems. Complex projects are intractable. They are emergent and unpredictable, driven by individual agendas and preferences. It is better to be present, sense what is going on and respond rather than relying on a detailed plan to direct activity. We need to move away from trying to predict and control the situation and put more effort into understanding what is occurring in order to influence the outcomes.

Even though scientific models don't work for complex projects, that doesn't mean we are left without any way of framing an approach. There are alternative thinking models that make sense when we talk about understanding and influence. Design thinking provides that alternative path, one that can inform an enhanced project toolkit.

Design thinking provides an alternative framing

Stop for a moment and reflect on what you think of when you hear the word 'design'. Most people turn their mind to graphics or fashion. More recently, you might think about well-designed products that have a visceral element, like those produced by Apple and Tesla.

While design as a concept isn't new, the use and awareness of design methods and tools outside 'pure' design domains has grown significantly over the past few years. Many people associate design thinking with either the common tools of the design (such as the use of visual representations, collaboration workshops with walls covered in Post-it notes, and prototyping, to name a few) or the underling human-centred approach (iterating answers with customers and developing journey maps). Some see it as just another problem-solving technique, with a focus on defining the problem well.

But design thinking is much more than that, because at its heart it is addressing a fundamentally different type of problem than science. To understand this, we need to head back further into the history of modern thought.

While the rise of science has a clear lineage to the Scientific Revolution and the Age of Enlightenment, the concepts upon which it was built date back to Ancient Greece. The core concepts of scientific knowledge have their roots in Aristotle's *Posterior Analytics* from around 350 BCE.[5]

Analytics is a way of comprehending 'what is'. It helps us to understand the world as it exists today – to discover an objective truth through rigorous examination, experimentation and distillation of an answer. The object being analysed doesn't change, even though our understanding of it might evolve. For example, changing our model from defining four elements of nature (earth, wind, fire and air) to the 118 elements of the periodic table didn't change the underlying nature of the world. Analytics is the foundation for scientific knowledge and explaining the physical world. It is occupied by questions like 'How far is it to the moon?' or 'How hot is it today?' It is focused on an external truth that is being discovered.

Unfortunately, analytics breaks down when dealing with objects that don't have a baseline truth to be discovered. It doesn't work for decisions that are just a matter of opinion, like choosing the most effective form of government, or the ideal place for a company retreat, or the best song in the world. Fortunately, Aristotle also had another body of work: rhetoric is the thinking model that is applied to things that don't have an inherent truth but are subjective and socially constructed. Rhetoric provides a framework for objects that can change based on choice. Analytics is fundamentally different to rhetoric (see Figure 4.1, over the page). Aristotle made the distinction that you can't have knowledge and opinion at the same time about the same thing.

In the rhetorical system, truth is subjective and created by the community, by those involved in the discourse at the time. With no external, technical reference to fall back on, individual perspectives define reality because they aren't constrained by the natural world. Truth is defined, not discovered. In this arena, emphasis is put on the role of intuition and the intent of the speaker. The skills of the participants centre on persuasion – the ability to understand the audience, question, listen, and put forward a logical and compelling argument.

Analytical thinking creates the ability to make a nuclear bomb, and rhetorical thinking underpins the decision to use it.

All this then leaves a question: if analytics came to underpin science as we know it today, where has rhetoric landed in the modern world?

Rhetoric's original focus was on the art of public speaking, and it is a clear ancestor of modern law and politics. A line can also be drawn to architecture and design, although this is hotly debated. Some academics describe rhetoric and design as 'two distinct fields of study intricately related'; others see rhetoric as actually a subset of design, because designed products persuade and influence us in a way that rhetoric does with words.[6]

Regardless of whether you perceive any formal link between rhetoric and design, they share significant similarities. The five canons of rhetoric deal with development of new ideas (invention), organising the ideas (arrangement), tone and manner (style), understanding of the topic (memory) and presentation (delivery). These clearly overlap with modern use of design methods.

More significantly, both rhetoric and design are based on a different frame of thinking to analytics and science, which can inform an alternative approach for dealing with the intractable nature of complex projects.

Figure 4.1: Analytics versus rhetoric

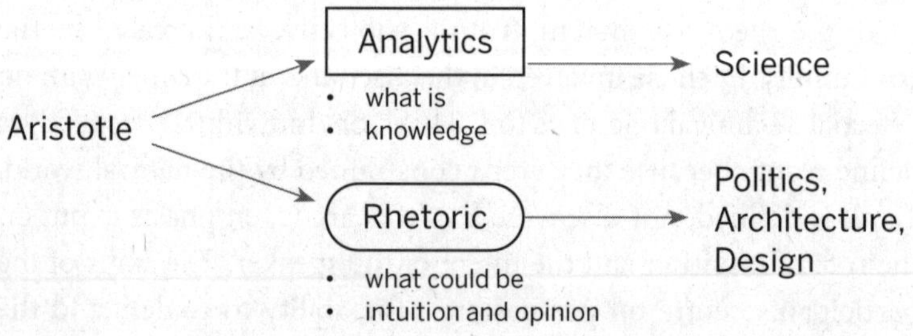

Design thinking defined

Whether it comes from rhetoric or is bigger than rhetoric, it is worthwhile being clear on what design thinking is. While rhetoric has a strong theoretical base, design thinking has many definitions available at the moment. It has variously been described as a disposition (Strom[7]), a system (Brown[8]) and a social technology (Liedtka[9]), among other things. This variance is because there isn't an agreed canon for design and design thinking; there is no single article or manifesto that can be referenced to frame any discussion (as there is for the Agile method, for example). While I don't pretend to have created an immutable definition of the topic, I have distilled it down to five themes that recur across the design thinking literature and practice. This classification helps to understand how design thinking differs from scientific thinking, how it is congruent with the characteristics of complexity and how it might inform an extended project toolkit.

The recurring themes are that design mindsets and practices are:

1. **Generative** – a focus on what could be
2. **Dialectical** – bringing together different opinions
3. **Intuitive** – the answer 'makes sense'
4. **Synthetic** – understanding and simplifying patterns in the whole system
5. **Responsive** – constantly changing, iterating towards a result.

Generative

Design thinking is about creating something new, not describing what already exists. Creativity and striving for relentless improvement are basic human traits, and generating a different future is both a personal and a collective activity based on the drive to make things better. With a sense of possibility and purpose, we take on big and complex challenges.

Design thinking focuses on understanding and solving a human need. It is about generating options and bringing to life new forms, informed but unencumbered by what already exists. It puts the opinions, desires and experiences of people at the very centre of the approach. This is why design activities are often referred to as 'human-centred' or 'user-centred'.

Dialectical

At the heart of design thinking is a dialogue, a conversation between different voices. Where science looks for consistency in detailed data for answers, design synthesises a multiplicity of voices. Design thinking actively brings in disparate points of view, and the more heterogeneous they are, the better and more nuanced the result. The dialogue is about surfacing different assumptions and interpretations to have a productive conversation and create shared meaning. It combines the ambition of the new CEO, the energy and fresh perspective of the recent graduate and the 'that will never work here' insights of the 30-year veteran to find a completely new take on the situation.

A large part of this dialogue is about not trying to resolve tensions immediately, but to let differences exist and look for the brilliance in each point of view. It is about creating 'with' rather than 'for' someone. Or, as Jeanne Liedtka from the Darden School at the University of Virginia puts it, 'design seeks to manage an ever present set of tensions like those between familiarity and novelty… exploration and exploitation.'[10]

Intuitive

Intuition is about finding a logical and consistent answer that 'makes sense' even if there isn't a clear cause-and-effect relationship or previous example to draw upon. The logic of this answer is supported by abductive reasoning. Abductive reasoning (see Box E) focuses on the most likely explanation or outcome for which there is no proof. It is what you believe to be true, or the

E: Abductive reasoning – logic without proof

Scientific knowledge is built on two types of logic: inductive and deductive reasoning.

> **Deductive:** All swans are white. This is a swan, therefore it is white.
>
> **Inductive:** Every time the doorbell rings the dog runs to the window, so the next time the doorbell rings the dog will run to the window.

Both of these forms of reasoning rely on proof, but they offer no new insights. They are also subject to breakdown if the model turns out to be wrong: all swans were white… until someone saw a black swan in Western Australia.

But what if there is no previous model that can be applied? What if you have an insight that no one else has? Abductive reasoning takes a set of observations and identifies the most likely explanation.

> **Abductive:** Of all the explanations, this one makes the most sense to me.

Introduced by American philosopher Charles Sanders Peirce, it is a logical inference, but unlike induction and deduction it is not tied to what has gone before.[11] Rather, it is based on the realisation that an observation doesn't fit the current models.

Abductive logic allows new insights to arise, and you can use it as reasonable grounds to get moving even when you don't have certainty. While it is based on the idea that something is true because you believe it to be true, it doesn't mean you can claim the Earth is flat just because you believe it. The outcome has to make sense based on all the available information, and the abductive hypothesis has to be testable.

Abductive reasoning is at the heart of creativity because it can bring in framings from completely different contexts. Induction and deduction stand on what has gone before as a basis of proof. This is why 'prove it' are two words that will kill off innovation – genuinely new ideas can't be proven deductively or inductively because there is no previous data.

best, or the most beautiful. It is an effective approach when dealing with topics with a range of perspectives and no clear answer.

Another critical element of abductive thinking is that, unlike inductive and deductive logic, it is not bound by what has gone before. It brings frames and ideas from disparate environments to create new understandings and open up new ways of thinking. Lionel March observes, 'A speculative design cannot be determined logically, because the mode of reasoning involved is essentially abductive.'[12]

Synthetic

In the mind of the designer, greater understanding comes from looking at the system as a whole and seeing how each of the parts combine and interact, rather than breaking the system down into its constituent parts. It is about identifying patterns and significant influences that explain the complete system rather than deep diving into individual components.

Mastery of science comes from focusing on more and more detail in a specific domain. Alternatively, design thinking generates value by bring together all the elements in the system and looking for overall patterns. The target outcome from design thinking is an elegant simplification, whether it be in a beautiful product or in the simple explanation of a complex situation.

Developing insights about the system involves developing ideas, checking them against concrete examples and using this experience to improve your ideas. Donald Schon described 'creating virtual worlds that act as learning laboratories'.[13] The lessons from this can then inform alternative paths of inquiry that will eventually be synthesised into an articulate view of the whole.

Responsive

Design thinking responds to the system as it emerges, as opposed to a scientific approach that looks to control the number of variables so the data produced is reliable and comparable. New information comes to light and new opinions arise, often only as a response to active investigation. Kurt Lewin famously said, 'you never really understand a system until you try and change it'. Emergence results from new data and insights that were either hidden or change as you intervene in the situation.

One of the implications of being responsive to the situation is that you need to keep your thinking flexible. You need to be willing to engage with what arises and take it on board. You can't just hold to a predefined path, because the new insights might need you to adjust your thinking, your approach or even your language.

An implication of being responsive is that revelations will continue to appear as you continue to expose new material and iterate towards something better. The choice becomes when to make the call to stop considering options and be satisfied with what you have. Responding to emergence is what creates uncertainty for those trying to manage the design process. Creativity and insight don't always work to a timetable, but we need to create the conditions to drive them forward because projects have to deliver results. But more on that later.

The centrality of learning and experimentation in design thinking requires curiosity and a willingness to suspend 'knowing the answer' in favour of integrating a range of views. It requires a willingness to allow the time for new insights to arise before converging upon an answer. This runs dramatically against the normal pressures of narrowing in on a solution as quickly as possible, locking in an answer and moving on to the next question. If you have ever worked with designers, this willingness to follow a range of paths before finally converging upon an answer is probably the most frustrating part of the process, particularly if you have a science or technical background (and to you the answer is obvious!). However, it is only in this willingness to sit with the problem – to look over the edges and see the connections – that we get to comprehend the whole system at work.

Comparison between science and design

These five themes of design (generative, dialectical, intuitive, synthetic and responsive) give a sense of how design thinking operates and how it approaches problems. Table 4.3 shows how design thinking brings a completely different lens to the situation when compared with the scientific approach discussed previously. Science is fundamentally about objective, external truth that can be proven, whereas design thinking defines a subjective truth based on exploration and learning. They are two alternative models for understanding the world.

Table 4.3: Comparison of scientific and design thinking themes

Scientific Thinking	⟷	Design Thinking
Descriptive What is	Focus of discovery	**Generative** What could be
Empirical The answer can be found in the data	Source of insight	**Dialectical** Disparate voices in tension create a more complete picture
Provable Using inductive or deductive logic based on what has gone before	System of reasoning	**Intuitive** Using abductive logic to explain or develop something new
Reductionist Understanding and mastery comes from increased detail	Nature of knowing	**Synthetic** Looking up and out, searching for patterns and simplicity
Replicable Conducting the same experiment will yield the same results	Attitude to change	**Responsive** Adapt as each iteration reveals new information

Design thinking works well in complexity

Design thinking is more than just a different lens. It is a more useful framing for complex projects.

Earlier in the chapter I showed how scientific thinking is incompatible with the characteristics of complexity – how the disdain for individual opinions and need for detailed proof runs against the nature of complex projects.

Alternatively, design thinking – with its focus on exploration and learning – is clearly aligned with these characteristics. For example, the dialectical nature of design brings multiple voices into the room, which makes it much easier to deal with a problem that is connected (where no one person has the answer) and subjective (where the answer changes with different perspectives). When the problem is unknowable, then an abductive approach can fill the gap until the answer emerges. Figure 4.2, over the page, maps the full extent of alignment between the complexity characteristics and the design thinking themes.

All of this means that design thinking provides a viable alternative upon which to build a toolkit for complex projects. It brings a framing that embraces complexity and all the messiness associated with it, and has proven itself in many other environments to be useful.

Successful in many domains

Design thinking is successful in highly ambiguous environments where there is no certainty of success. The success of graphic design and product design depends on the reaction of an audience. The commercial impact of launching an innovative product is unknowable until it is in the market. There are no rules for the size of a new TV or the font on a menu. There are methods for discovery and prototyping, but ultimately the decisions are driven by opinions and by style. Despite all this uncertainty, the designer's toolkit has been successful in navigating these unknowns.

There are domains beyond just graphic design and product design in which design thinking is successful. Richard Buchanan, a leading academic on design thinking, described two additional areas: Interaction and Systems design. The first focuses on activities and process leading to the design of services and experiences. The second is broader again, looking at entire systems such as organisations and government. Both Interaction and Systems design have grown rapidly over the past few years on the back of user-centred design techniques, workshops and training courses.

Design thinking has also been applied to activities beyond these areas, such as business strategy development. This is based on the view that strategy is ambiguous and you can't analyse your way to a different future – that it is a creative, emergent activity.

Figure 4.2: Alignment of complexity characteristics and design themes

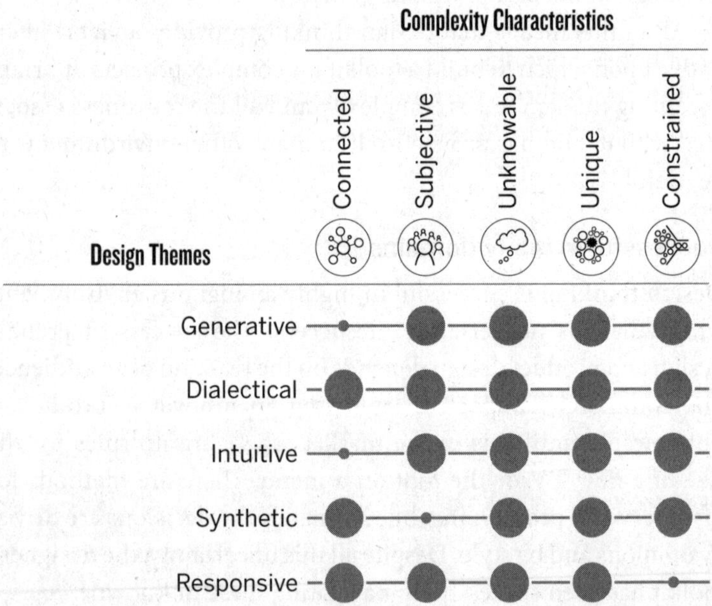

So, the idea of using design thinking beyond just graphic and product design is not new. What is new is applying it to complex projects in a comprehensive way. This is about applying the mindsets and methods of a proven way of thinking across the whole domain of project management to lift performance.

Successful in project management

The design thinking approach has proven to be successful in projects, not just in requirements-gathering workshops or user-design sessions but in the way projects are managed and led.

Alexis was a great designer with whom I worked on a large project. The project had a room where all of the workstreams displayed their status reports on the wall. Unfortunately, all the reports were presented in a different format, so it was difficult to assess and compare performance quickly. I asked Alexis to make them all the same so they would be easy to comprehend quickly. Her response was to ask: Why do we need them? Why do they exist? How did they end up this way? What conversation occurs around these reports?

This clearly shows the mind of the designer at work; this is what good designers do. While scientists drill down into a problem, designers step back and take a broader view. I just wanted the reports to all look the same so they were easier to read, but she saw the need to look at the whole system and question why people were producing the status reports at all. If we just standardised the reports, the workstream managers would continue to fill them out. However, if the project managers understood why the interaction was required, they would make the reports easy to understand and less effort to produce, creating more clarity. Bringing the design mindset to this problem wasn't about making the reports easier to read: it was about making them useful, and ensuring the managers didn't feel they were wasting their time and the executives had their questions answered.

This is what sets designers apart from technical thinkers. I just wanted the problem fixed; she questioned if I was focusing on the right problem. I saw layout and readability problems; she saw information flows and social interactions. This is both brilliant and frustrating. All I wanted was a simple solution because the project was complex and under massive time pressure, but she was forcing me to question my thinking.

If we had only standardised the reports then any poor reporting behaviours that existed would have continued, just with a common layout. Instead, taking the time to understand the purpose of the status reporting and redesign the whole interaction gave ownership of the process to each of the workstream leaders. The reporting moved from a weekly 'tick a box' activity with standard responses to a deeper conversation, and a willingness to address the real progress and risks in the emerging situation.

When you take on a design-driven approach, you need to be willing to open up a bigger conversation that improves the performance of the project, rather than just fixing one particular situation.

Scientific or design approach?

Here is a simple test. Reflect on the best project you have worked on. Was the best thing about the project that the detailed plan and regular status reports provided predictability and control? Or was it taking on something difficult and uncertain, engaging with people, experimenting and constantly learning, immersed in a sense of possibility? If you reflect on it, you'll probably find that the design thinking themes make sense from your experience.

Taking a design-based approach is not easy. For many years, our approach to project management has stood upon the belief that everything can be modelled and predicted – that you can lay out a plan and measure performance against it. A design thinking approach will drive you to give up on this idea and bring forward a more realistic framing of the situation, instead of creating a sense that you have the situation under control when, in reality, you don't.

I know I'm asking you to suspend a lifetime of experience and try another way. I respect that it's a difficult thing to do, but the design thinking model does work. If you want to go down this path, it's important that you don't just accept the shortcomings of the standard toolkit. The Complex Project Toolkit is not about abandoning what we know but adding to what exists.

Take a moment to look at where you see breakdowns in the projects you have underway. It might be that you are getting mixed messages about progress, or sensible but questionable explanations for all of the time slippages that occur, or just a nagging feeling that something is missing. Consider whether these issues could be caused by an incomplete toolkit. Have confidence that moving to a design-based approach is based on solid theory, evidence, experience and clear thinking, and could lift the performance of these projects.

Design thinking offers a way to manage complex projects without taming them too early or straitjacketing them into a fixed plan. Using a toolkit based on design thinking will better match a situation that presents itself in complexity. It will alleviate the stress on the people involved and improve project results. We can put down the hammer and use a screwdriver that is fit for purpose and does exactly what it's supposed to do. But this does require a new toolkit with different mindsets, practices and skills. This is where the Complex Project Toolkit comes in.

Part II

THE COMPLEX PROJECT TOOLKIT

Chapter 5

A DESIGN-DRIVEN PROJECT TOOLKIT

'If you want to succeed you should strike out on new paths, rather than travel the worn paths of accepted success.'
—John D. Rockefeller

So, the standard toolkit is ineffective in complexity because of its underlying mental model, and design thinking has a strong alignment with the characteristics of complexity. But it is not enough just to notice this alignment. What do we do with this insight? The real question is, how does the project management approach and toolkit need to change to improve our success rate with complexity?

The Complex Project Toolkit, informed by design thinking, is based on a new narrative for projects. It is a shift away from the mechanistic paradigm focused on prediction and control that is inherent in the standard toolkit. It moves instead towards a more emergent method that is motivated by understanding and continuous learning. It is not just a few extra lines on a status report or a new workshop to add during project startup; it is much broader than that. The toolkit consists of new mindsets, practices and skills that create an enhanced project management approach.

- **Mindsets** are what we believe and what drive our behaviour. The toolkit requires a fundamental shift in our relationship with certainty and predictability. It is about embracing ambiguity and having a different perspective on learning. Different mindsets lead to new ways of operating and underpin the new practices.
- **Practices** are the activities that manage the complexity of the situation without taming it too early. They are not rigid processes but rather generic ways of working that improve effectiveness in complexity and are supported by new skills.
- **Skills** are the capabilities required to deliver this new way of working and generate understanding and movement, even when the path is unclear. Many models for complexity describe new capabilities required at a very high level – for example, 'innovation' and 'strategic thinking'. The skills identified in the Complex Project Toolkit are much more atomic than that – questioning, listening, reframing. They are capabilities not normally associated with project managers but are straight out of the designer's toolkit.

Table 5.1 compares the operating model of the standard toolkit with the Complex Project Toolkit. The intent is not to throw out what already exists, because the standard project management tools and techniques are effective and work well for normal projects. Rather, the Complex Project Toolkit is an enhanced way of working that drives performance when elements of a project are complex. It brings together a collaborative, emergent approach and the hard-edged delivery focus required in projects. It is a coherent model that doesn't try to tame ambiguity, but rather coexists with it until it falls to a level at which the normal approach can cope.

Table 5.1: Project management models

	Standard Toolkit	Complex Project Toolkit
MINDSETS	Focus on what to deliver Draw on expertise Documentation is critical Control the process Detail creates clarity Minimise change	Keep asking why Give up knowing Always curious There is no certainty Step back, look up Choose your own path
PRACTICES	Scope Plan Track Adjust Communicate	Connect Simplify Hold space Find a way Believe
SKILLS	Communication Planning and scheduling Measuring and controlling	Conversation Sense-making Adaption

The Complex Project Toolkit represents a project management model designed to be effective when dealing with the characteristics of complexity outlined in Chapter 2.

The model isn't prescriptive in nature because each complex project will be different. It provides overall guidelines and heuristics that are more effective in complexity than detailed and dogmatic methods. It focuses on the areas that offer the highest leverage and are easiest to implement, and allows each organisation or individual to adjust it to suit their situation.

Within this new approach, fresh ways of operating arise: the plan becomes a thinking tool rather than a tracking document, and the governance meetings focus on what we need to learn rather than describing what happened.

As shown in Figure 5.1, high performance comes when all the elements of the toolkit are aligned. Without alignment across all areas of the toolkit, there will be predictable breakdowns that degrade performance:

- **Ineffective gathering** occurs when you understand the practices and take on the mindsets but don't take the time to build the required skills. You will get moving, but progress will be slow because any activity will be ineffective, with participants having all the will but none of the skill.
- **Lip service** occurs when teams agree to adopt the practices and build the skills but don't take on the mindsets. The result is that activities will occur, but they won't last because there is no belief in the new way of working. The first sign of difficulty will send everyone back to their old approaches.
- **Sporadic brilliance** occurs when you adopt the mindsets and skills but don't embrace the new practices. Your team will understand the value of the toolkit and have the skills to implement it, but there will be no organising methods to their activities. Without the framing to guide their actions, results won't be reliable; instead, they will rely on individual performance to extract value.

Figure 5.1: Outcomes of the Complex Project Toolkit

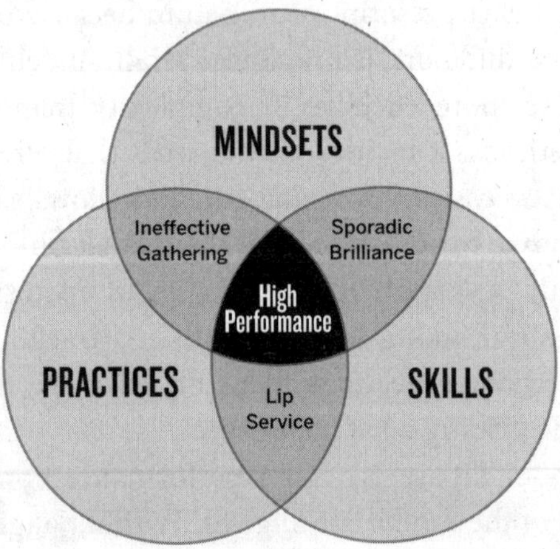

It is a comprehensive model

The Complex Project Toolkit is applicable to a greater range of projects and issues than other models used to address uncertainty in projects. The most common models are stage gates and iterative methods.

Stage gates

Stage gates are identified checkpoints in a project where progress is reviewed and decisions are made about proceeding to the next stage of the project. They are designed to release funding and approval progressively as more information is accumulated. When you are trying to get your project approved, they make it clear what hoops you need to jump through to get the next round of funding. They limit the scope of any potential downside until things are known. But they don't deal with complexity; they don't address the wickedness driven by different agendas. This is just a progressive decision model laid over the top of the standard model to limit project runaway.

Front-end loading is a form of stage-gating and is another well-known project management technique used in capital-intensive developments. It is about bringing forward the design and key decisions to drive out uncertainties that might occur later in the project. All the critical decisions are made upfront before progressing to the next stage of the project. It doesn't deal with unknowable issues or emergence, focusing only on reducing the likelihood of expensive technical changes later in the project.

This technique was used by the builder who renovated my house. They made sure all the design decisions were made before work started, even down to the choice of taps, tiles and doorknobs. This ensured the project was delivered on time. But this approach would not have been so successful if the work had to be stopped because a neighbour complained, because it isn't designed for complexity.

Iterative methods

Iterative project management methods like Spiral and Agile have been very successful and progressively develop the final solution, but they do it within a very bounded system. These methods are useful in projects where changes are easily made, such as process design or software development, and when there is clarity on what needs to be developed, but there are a few issues with these approaches in complex projects.

Firstly, once the path is set, they are unwilling to consider alternative macro-level approaches. Agile is not set up to question the strategy or change the context. If the focus of the team is on implementing a new widget, then they will find the fastest and most productive way to produce the widget. They will iterate towards the best widget, getting feedback and occasionally throwing out bits of the widget for an improved piece. However, they will never consider if a new doohickie would have been a better way to deliver the outcome.

The second issue is that Agile works to 'name and tame' the situation quickly by using deliverables to confirm requirements and deliver the highest possible value in the first release – but never questioning if the right problem is being solved or if critical assumptions are incorrect. This is because it iterates 'design and build' cycles towards a solution and assumes the problem has been accurately defined. However, as Rittel points out, when you take action in wickedness you change the nature of the problem, so any effective approach in complexity needs to be able to change direction to solve a different problem.[1]

Finally, a major focus of the Agile method is to keep moving forward. Sometimes projects need a reverse gear when they hit issues. In complex projects it is possible that, as more becomes known about the situation, the original piece delivered a few months ago no longer matches the situation. Sometimes you need to refocus effort on an entirely different issue or roadblock. Agile is not designed to backtrack and throw out large amounts of what has already been supplied. Imagine a negotiation in which you get close to the end of the discussions and then everything is overturned because of a single issue, or the deal you thought was done breaks down at the last moment; iterative techniques don't provide a method for dealing with this type of complexity.

Some elements of iterative approaches are recognisable in the Complex Project Toolkit. Agile, for example, encourages responding to change and regular interactions between team members. However, this doesn't make them immediately comparable. The Complex Project Toolkit addresses more of the social wickedness inherent in complexity and draws on a range of design thinking models to be effective in a greater range of situations.

Design thinking models provide a way of operating within complexity and focus on making sure the right problem is being addressed. Design thinking frameworks – such as Stanford University's d.school model, with its focus on exploration and ideation, or the Double Diamond method (see Box F, overleaf) – give prominence to generating the most learning as early as possible and confirming the right problem is being addressed. The Double Diamond method embodies the divergence and convergence inherent in design approaches, where there is a willingness to explore multiple lines of inquiry before uniting at an answer. Other models depict the circular rather than linear experience of problem definition and solution. The implication of a design-based approach is that a project creates more questions and more uncertainty to begin with, but will eventually move through complexity to clarity.

Don't replace the traditional approach – augment it

The point of the Complex Project Toolkit is not to discard all the disciplines of standard project management, but rather to augment them with additional capabilities informed by design thinking that embrace inherent ambiguity. These new ideas need to be woven into the toolkit of project managers to be used as required.

F: Double Diamond model of design thinking

While there are many different design thinking models, the Double Diamond (see Figure 5.2) captures some of the concepts of design thinking.[2] The key elements of the model are:

- **Divergence and convergence:** The diamonds represent a process of diverging from the immediate and searching beyond the normal scope. The divergence collects more information and also might raise new questions not previously considered, before then converging upon an answer.
- **Problem definition before solution:** The first diamond converges to the definition of the problem, also referred to as 'problem finding', before diverging again and then coming back to the final solution.

Chapter 3 described the ineffectiveness of rushing to deliver an answer. This model shows how moving as quickly as possible towards the answer gives no space for confirming the right problem is being addressed.

Because iterative methods such as Agile use each iteration to get closer to the answer, they don't involve a search away from what we know. Agile is shown in the 'deliver' phase of the Double Diamond. It is not designed to check if the right problem is being solved, only to progressively move towards a solution.

Figure 5.2: The Double Diamond model

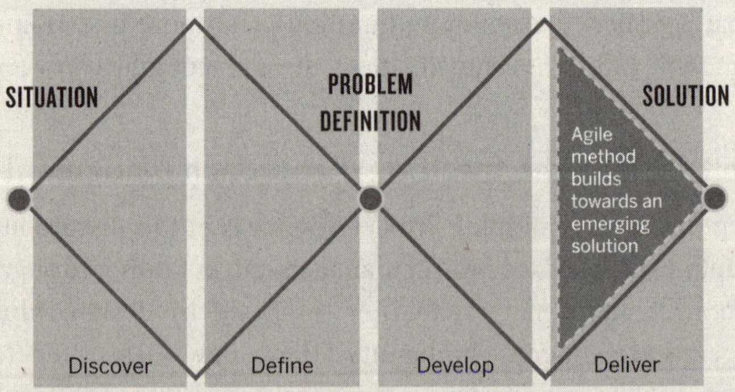

In complex projects, the role of the project manager changes to one of creating understanding and promoting learning across the team and with stakeholders.

With an understanding of the nature of project complexity (from Chapter 2) you are already on the way to improving performance in your projects. The next step is to understand the components of the Complex Project Toolkit and how to adopt this new way of working. It is a new narrative that goes beyond the original project management methods when complexity demands it.

Proven to work

This toolkit works. The techniques have underpinned the acceleration of many project deliveries. A design-based approach will fundamentally change the attitude and interactions among everyone involved in your complex project. It will create real conversations, and they will probably be uncomfortable, but you will tackle the things that stand in the way of success. It will expose the messiness inherent in complexity.

This toolkit will increase the chance of your project having a great outcome. On a large system development I worked on, it freed up the team to see a different approach and deliver the project at less than half the original budget. The price you pay for this improvement, and the obstacle to overcome when taking this on, is having to be open to an alternative way of working and give up the illusion of control that characterises the standard approach.

I have seen people move from frustration to calmness in complexity using the techniques of the Complex Project Toolkit. It can reinforce a leader's desire to get things done 'against the odds'. It may decrease certainty in the moment, but it provides a greater chance of success and reduces the level of wasted effort and frustration. Embracing this toolkit will enhance the joy of building something with others, even in stressful situations. The Complex Project Toolkit turns what could be debilitating experiences into memorable acts of creation.

Chapter 6
MINDSETS FOR COMPLEXITY

'Mindsets frame the running account that's taking place in people's heads. They guide the whole interpretation process.'
—Carol Dweck[1]

Your mindset is your attitude towards a situation. It filters everything you see and informs how you interpret the world; it affects how you react to situations and interact with people. The need for new mindsets in project management became obvious to me when I saw project managers responding unsuccessfully to situations. They would hold fast to a schedule despite the team not believing it was possible, use the contract as a decision tool for any uncertainty or assume everyone had the same understanding of a situation. Their behaviours made sense to them, but clearly they were based on futile ways of thinking about issues. Without a different way of interpreting complexity, project managers will continue to believe they need to be the expert, to hold defined positions rather than opening up to the ideas of others and to be ineffective in complexity.

The mindsets required to succeed in complexity are significantly different from those of the standard project management toolkit discussed in Chapter 1. They require a fundamental shift in your relationship with certainty and predictability. Through research, experience and lessons from design thinking models, the Complex Project Toolkit identifies six mindsets that bring forward effective behaviours and ways of operating to strengthen performance in complex projects.

Taking on these mindsets means asking bigger questions, looking for alternative realities beyond your own experience and giving up on the fruitless drive for control. It's about embracing ambiguity and learning from it, rather than trying to drive out uncertainty as quickly as possible.

Your mindsets motivate your behaviours and actions. Understanding behaviour is a complex topic. The reality is that behaviour is influenced by much more than just mindsets – personality and environment have a big impact. The emphasis on mindsets alone in the Complex Project Toolkit is to focus on a particular element that we can work on. Mindsets are also easier to articulate and adjust than many other behavioural drivers.

The mindsets of the Complex Project Toolkit are connected, relying on and reinforcing each other. As you will see later in this chapter, they can all be juxtaposed against the mechanistic mindsets of the standard project management approach to show the significant difference in the mental model required to succeed in complex projects.

The six mindsets of the Complex Project Toolkit, shown in Figure 6.1, represent alternative expectations and interpretations of what occurs in complex projects.

Figure 6.1: Mindsets of the Complex Project Toolkit

Keep asking why

Have you ever heard a consultant or executive say the objective is to become a 'digital organisation'? 'We're going to have machine learning; we're going to have artificial intelligence… and drones, we're definitely going to use drones… and virtual reality.' What does it all mean?

When faced with such a challenge, the standard project management approach is to focus on the scope and the deliverables. When the situation is not well understood, it is easy to ask, 'What do you want me to deliver?' It bounds the problem and creates clarity.

Focusing on 'what' concentrates your attention on a solution. However, this is a problem in complexity, because in an attempt to create certainty, the objective of the project becomes confused with the object to be delivered.

The problem with focusing on deliverables in complexity is that it tames the problem too quickly. As the situation emerges, as understanding improves along the way, the notion of what the right answer is will change. If the intent of the project is defined by 'stuff' to be delivered, it is difficult to adjust when new information arises. Don't start with the answer; let it emerge.

In complexity, where even the definition of the problem can change, it is more important to attend to why the action is underway. 'Why' broadens your sights and opens up possibilities. A focus on 'what' should be delivered ensures you produce as per the original idea, but it might not be what is required or the best way to achieve the desired outcome. 'Why' gets you thinking about customers, staff, stakeholders and the community. 'Why' supports 'problem finding', where you make sure you are working on the most valuable problem with the best approach.

I've seen a $2 million software implementation cancelled in favour of a $200,000 process change to solve an insurance company reconciliation issue, because the project team stood back and asked 'why'. Why are we doing this project? Why is this the best way to achieve that outcome? The team had become so focused on the original solution that they lost sight of the overall intent. Being willing to continually focus on 'why' reinforces your ability to rethink the approach and find a better way in the middle of the project.

The other subtle but significant point to acknowledge is that anything worth doing is going to be difficult, and you will hit roadblocks along the way. Understanding 'why' sustains effort through uncertainty and doubt better than understanding 'what'. If the predefined contraption you need to deliver no longer fits the requirement or becomes too hard to follow through with, it is easy to become disheartened by the project. Also, when you're focused on the stuff to be delivered, you're missing the social aspect, the wickedness, the connectedness. If you define the project in terms of the object to be delivered, then when the going gets tough the team focuses more and more on just delivering the object rather than addressing the wider issues.

If you understand 'why', and you believe in it, then you will own the result – you will push through and find a way to make it happen, even if the final object that gets delivered has to change.

Give up knowing

If you have travelled much by rail, you'll be familiar with the 'whine' of the electric motor as the train accelerates. It can be loud and unpleasant, and is something that should be avoided when designing a new train. I witnessed the first test of a new motor in which the whine was disturbingly loud. The engineering manager said this wasn't a problem because it was an 'unloaded' test – it was a test of the separate traction assembly and didn't have a 400-tonne train on top of it. He said it probably wouldn't make any noticeable sound under normal conditions. The project manager saw the test result as a huge problem because of the likely customer reaction to motor-whine.

A meeting was arranged to bring the team together to decide whether or not they had a problem. The engineering manager contended it was not an issue. The project manager insisted it was a huge problem. Each vehemently argued their position, unwilling to consider any alternative. The meeting soon descended into chaos and the managers stormed out of the room without a resolution or any agreed action, each convinced he was right and any other interpretation was wrong.

The reality was that both were right, but being 'the expert' makes you blind to other options. When it comes to complexity, where perspectives define reality, there is no single truth – the answer is in the people involved and their opinions. We have to be willing to hear what others have to say. This is particularly hard when you are 'the expert'.

To 'give up knowing' is to relinquish the role of the expert to the group. If you give up knowing the answer, remove attachment to any particular position and become curious, your job as project manager becomes one of generating understanding in the team and trusting that they will work out the answer. As long as you maintain the role of the expert and believe you have the only answer, you diminish your chance of hearing others. The project manager's job is to lead the discovery, look for the brilliance in others and bring everyone together through questioning rather than being the source of the answer.

Complexity is characterised by a high level of unknowns – not just unknowns that require a more detailed Google search, but things no one can answer yet. We don't know how customers will react in the moment; we don't know what employees will say when they have to make significant decisions. No single person has the answer, so it has to come from the group. Competence is a collective capability, and knowledge is created through conversation between the players. The answer emerges from the specific situation with the particular people who are present, and therefore everyone should be heard.

Going back to the motor-whine example, if at least one of the managers had given up being the expert and listened, there would have been a chance to move forward and address both the perception and the reality of the issue. Through asking good questions and taking the time to understand, with input from those around the room that day, an answer that worked for everyone could have emerged.

Willingly giving up being the expert is not normal behaviour for many project managers. However, the ability to ask good questions and compile a coherent argument based on the knowledge you acquire is an important skill for project managers in complexity.

In the most extreme form, to 'give up knowing' can also be to 'come from nothing'. This is when you don't hold any perceived opinions, biases or beliefs. This might be possible for a few very practised spiritual beings, but in most day-to-day operations it is impossible to come from nothing. It is possible, though, to be aware of the mindset you bring, understand your own biases and avoid the automatic 'click-whirr' response when things happen.

Here is a quick check for you to perform. How often while reading this book have you thought to yourself, 'That's wrong'? It is impossible to create space for new ideas to emerge if you believe you already have the answer. You have to be genuinely open to the opinions of others. In fact, a good test of your openness is to entertain two opposing opinions at once. Are you able to make the argument for both sides of a discussion? Making the case for another person, particularly if you don't agree with them, requires you to be empathetic and a very good listener (more on that in Chapter 8).

The desire to be right is powerful, particularly in technical environments, which makes this a difficult mindset to adopt. Most people in senior positions see their role as knowing more than others; it is a really important part of their status and position. This can cloud their judgement and lead to broader issues, as I saw on the train development project.

If you genuinely find it too hard to give up knowing and always feel the need to put your point of view forward, then consider the Dunning–Kruger effect. This research found that people with low capability in a subject often overestimate their ability and rush to put forward their point of view. More significantly, the real experts in a field will underestimate the level of their ability compared with others and therefore are more willing to listen.[2]

Giving up playing the expert doesn't mean you become passive. Rather, you replace a desire to show your expertise with a desire to learn and understand.

Always curious

I worked on an engineering site that had very expensive work rosters. Anyone could walk in and within a day see that the 12-hour shifts didn't match the work demand, accrued unnecessary penalty costs and clearly should be adjusted. But that diagnosis ignored the complexity of the situation. To understand why an unproductive roster had been in place for more than 20 years, you needed to look deeper. With a bit of digging, you would discover that a staff vote was required to change any roster. So why hadn't they voted for a change? Talking to the frontline staff, it became obvious that many of them travelled long distances to work. The particular roster they had settled on had the least number of work days in a year; any other roster would increase the time they spent commuting. You might be able to prove it was an unproductive roster, but the whole ecosystem would resist any attempt to change it.

Complex projects have a web of connections, and as a project manager you need a nuanced understanding of the entire picture. This requires a view across the whole system, but also the curiosity to go 'five layers down' to really understand what's going on. High-level overviews and their resulting actions are ineffective in complexity. You need to understand why the situation is as it is. You need to be willing to ask 'dumb' questions to see the connections. You need to get into the detail, genuinely listen and empathise to have any chance of generating insight or delivering results. You need to let curiosity drive you to go beyond the superficial, to understand the human stories as well as the data.

In complexity, where perspectives define reality and many things are unknowable, an inquiring mind and a desire for understanding is critical to operate effectively. This is because information is emergent and not readily available at the beginning of the project. The best answer is rarely obvious; it evolves and emerges as understanding increases. Iteration and reflection are essential, because you're unlikely to get any answer right the first time.

It can also take time for your creative and insightful engine to kick into gear. I've always found it takes at least three versions of an answer before a good one appears. You need to sit with the problem and not feel the need to solve it immediately. This runs against the common practice in projects of quickly identifying answers because you don't have time to iterate and you have to keep moving forward.

Curiosity doesn't stop just because you find an answer. Maintaining curiosity means you don't get attached to a hypothesis, even one you came up with yourself. Treat it as only the current point of view, a way station in the pursuit of knowledge. The belief that you have found the answer gets in the way of real curiosity.

Look to break rather than prove your view. Carl Sagan in his book *The Demon-Haunted World* suggests you 'ask yourself why you like the idea. Compare it fairly with alternatives. See if you can find reasons for rejecting it. If you don't, others will.'[3] In complexity, most things are up for debate.

If you are being truly curious and driving for understanding, then contention within the team is something to be encouraged. You need a willingness to listen when issues arise, because they can reveal critical information.

The development of the Airbus A380 was delayed by two years from the original launch date and incurred billions of dollars of extra cost due to a range of issues, including mismatches in the design between different suppliers. The issues were first mentioned in late 2004 but were not acknowledged, at least not publicly, for another six months.[4] An unwillingness to be curious, to be open to the idea that significant issues could arise, only masked the problem until it got to a point where it could no longer be ignored. If you are going to be genuinely curious, then you need to be comfortable with the idea of failure, the idea that your curiosity might uncover something you would prefer not to know (see Box G).

If you are in a culture where you aren't allowed to make any mistakes, then all you are doing is saving up problems until they can't be hidden anymore, at which point they will be revealed in one big breakdown that will be impossible or really expensive to fix.

G: Curiosity and a relationship to failure

To be truly curious you can't be afraid of failure. You have to be okay with asking the wrong question, or coming up with the wrong suggestion, or hearing things you didn't want to hear. Young children represent the pinnacle of curiosity, unconstrained by any fear of how they might be perceived or what the answer might entail.

Being curious, trying out different things and being willing to move without full information will lead to errors, and errors are full of information. If everything is going well, then you are not learning much at all. If something is going wrong, then the curious will ask, 'How do I learn from this?'

When I worked at Hewlett-Packard, we were made aware that there are three ways you can approach customer feedback, with the third being most effective:

1. Avoid – it represents a failure and creates more work.
2. Respond – keep the customer happy.
3. Actively seek – use it to improve the way you do things.

Clearly the third option surfaces more issues but also leads to greater understanding and an improved ability to operate well. However, if you are actively seeking feedback, you need to be ready for responses that might be uncomfortable and willing to have those difficult conversations. If you are being curious then you need to be open to being told about what is going wrong, even if you have a different opinion about what the points of failure are.

There is also a relationship between our attitude towards failure and the 'growth mindset' described by Carol Dweck in her book *Mindset*. A fixed mindset sees capability as preordained and static, so any failure is interpreted as a lack of capability. Someone with a growth mindset believes capabilities are cultivated and that any issue means learning, not failing.

When failure is framed as another step on the journey of learning, it feeds the curiosity that drives the learning process. In complex projects, leaders have to build the space for the team to be curious without a fear of failure.

There is no certainty

The standard project management approach uses documentation, plans, risk management processes and status reporting to create certainty about costs, deliverables and timelines. In complexity, however, the emergent nature of the situation, driven by individual perspectives and unknowables, means there is no certainty and things can change at a moment's notice. This mindset allows you to accept this situation rather than trying to create certainty where it doesn't exist.

Taking on this mindset in complexity produces an interesting result. By giving up on the need to create the appearance of certainty and always be in control, you free the team to focus on the outcome. Less time is spent on maintaining consistency from one report to the next; the emphasis is on where we are going and what we have learned, rather than on making sure that the previous approach and estimates were correct.

If there is no certainty, then the focus turns to sensing and responding as you learn. The plan is no longer a tracking document but a thinking tool that outlines the latest understanding. Learning becomes important because no one knows for sure how things will end up. This mindset demands that the approach be adjusted as the situation changes. The answer is just the current point of view, not something carved in stone.

This mindset is not without some downsides. Without certainty, resilience becomes important. As humans, we crave certainty and try to remove uncertainty. David Rock, the founding president of the NeuroLeadership Institute, talks about how 'uncertainty registers (in a part of the brain called the anterior cingulate cortex) as an error, gap, or tension: something that must be corrected before one can feel comfortable again.'[5]

But, in a strange twist, when we recognise uncertainty it can trigger our interest. Rock goes on to write, 'New and challenging situations create a mild threat response, increasing levels of adrenaline and dopamine just enough to spark curiosity and energize people to solve problems.' In an overlap with the previous mindset, cultivating curiosity makes us more resilient to uncertainty.

In uncertainty, ways of working become less prescriptive and more reactive. If things are stable and repeatable, as they are in normal operations, routines can be detailed and trusted to work. Eisenhardt and Martin talk about how, as uncertainty increases, the ways of working become 'more simple and experiential, and their outcomes more unpredictable'.[6]

I ran a workshop in an engineering organisation to define a recovery plan for a project that was in trouble. My intent was to conduct it as a conversation and see what topics emerged from the discussion, to understand what was important to the leadership team. The person organising the day wanted an agenda that defined the order of topics to be discussed and when the plan would come together. I saw this as unnecessary, because it was going to be an exploration of their world in a free-flowing discussion, but she was persistent. So, I agreed to provide a run sheet for the day, showing the order of topics to be discussed, but had no intention of sticking to it. In the morning session, we covered a wide range of issues by asking some simple questions that opened up the conversation. It was clear that people were really passionate about particular topics, and many of those topics weren't on the agenda. At lunchtime, the organiser was worried about how it was all going to come together and that we had diverged significantly from the agenda. The conversation was synthesised in the afternoon and the strategy reflected a number of significant themes that weren't on the radar before the start of the session. In being open to uncertainty and allowing the discussion to move towards what was important, the team built a recovery plan that they believed in because it focused on the most significant issues that were revealed.

Step back, look up

How would you describe sugar? You could take the scientific approach and describe it as a combination of carbon, hydrogen and oxygen atoms in the ratio $C_nH_{2n}O_n$ with 'n' being between 3 and 7. Actually it is the monosaccharides that take this form, but there are also disaccharides and oligosaccharides. This is what you do with a scientific mindset – go into detail to understand something. Alternatively, you could step back and see how sugar is used, and just describe it as sweet. This is the difference between reductionist thinking, which understands something by pulling it apart into its component pieces, and 'synthetic' thinking, which looks to comprehend the whole situation by looking at the object and its context.

Synthetic thinking is more effective in complexity because of the connectedness of the topics. Diving into technical detail causes confusion, because trying to understand a specific point when there is a lack of clear boundaries between topics leaves you feeling that there is much more to know.

To understand complexity, you need to constantly step back and take a wider view, seeing the whole system and understanding the broader interactions and connections to other issues. Focusing on the detail can lead you to miss important influences that are visible only from a distance. Clarity comes from looking at the bigger picture.

This mindset drives you to change your focus from 'down in the detail' to 'up and out'. The more you lift your thinking out of the detail and focus on the overall ambition, the more you can take action that has real impact on the entire situation. Stepping back to maintain perspective on the overall ambition also builds resilience, because the bigger picture remains constant as everything else changes, often in unpredictable ways.

To generate understanding, designers use diagrams and metaphors to create insight by looking at the situation through a different lens. They search for the reframing that gives them the best access to the problem. It takes time to do this well – to create a simple yet insightful description. This reframing is only possible if you step back and take in the whole landscape of the complex project, rather than focusing on getting specific technical details right.

Synthesising the whole situation into a simple 'map of the territory' makes complexity manageable; this is discussed in detail in the next chapter. A well-constructed diagram or insightful naming makes it easier for people to understand their role and how their actions contribute to the outcome in what is an unclear and interconnected environment.

This mindset drives you to identify which areas are the most significant and where to focus your curiosity. Curiosity motivates you to understand the whole situation – technical, social and environmental – and can lead you to dive into details, but if you are being curious then you have to occasionally step back to make sure you are putting effort into the right areas. A simple technique to make sure this happens is to take a blank sheet of paper, sit in a coffee shop and see what thoughts emerge. Removing yourself from the day-to-day and giving yourself space to think often brings forward insights that help you make sure you are still on the right path.

Choose your own path

In his 2018 book *The Wizard and the Prophet*, Charles Mann proposes that the world is made up of two types of people: wizards, who see possibility everywhere and believe we can think our way out of our constraints, often with the use of new technologies; and prophets, who see the world as constrained, and believe resources are limited and we have to live within those limits.[7] Many project managers tend to be prophets, seeing the project constraints as a given and the approach as locked in, so the plan should be delivered as agreed. You will be more effective in complex projects if you are a wizard, seeing possibility all around you and rethinking the approach to get to the outcome in the best possible way.

'Choose your own path' stands upon the belief that you have power over the situation, and you get to design all the elements of it. This is possible in complexity because the context is malleable – the situation is created by opinions and perspectives, not ordained by some power beyond our understanding.

While the standard project mindset looks to minimise changes, this mindset is about understanding the reality of constraints and changing things to achieve the outcome in the best possible way. Given that most constraints aren't real (as shown in Chapter 2) and opinions define the situation, this provides you with almost complete freedom to design the system. While the funding may be limited, it's often not as inflexible as people assume, and there is liberty to influence stakeholders and adjust the way the project is governed.

The belief that you are unable to make the call to do things differently is the biggest roadblock to this mindset. How often have you heard, 'It's above my pay grade'? This is the language of someone being a victim to the situation.

The willingness to choose your own path is essential for the 'Find a way' practice described in the next chapter. Complex projects are emergent – you have to be ready to question the status quo, to always look for a better way, rather than continue to waste time on a trajectory that is either inefficient or has no hope of delivering the outcome.

If you don't like the situation, change it. Are you willing to make your own way in the world without being bound by what others might say or believe? All of this is driven by the conviction that the result is worth more than the potential downside of speaking out. Are you really willing to seek forgiveness rather than ask permission? If the project is going poorly, you get to choose to make it great.

The new mindsets might appear relatively simple. Maybe you have come across some of them in contexts other than project management. Not all of these mindsets are in play all the time – sometimes you need to be curious; sometimes you need to define a new way of approaching the problem. The point is that they are a new way of thinking that improves the delivery of your hardest projects.

Comparing with the standard mindsets

The mindsets required in complex projects differ markedly from those in the standard project approach. To recap, Chapter 1 introduced the six standard project mindsets developed during the industrial origins of project management. A comparison with them is shown in Table 6.1.

The standard mindsets frame the situation as predictable and controllable. The attitude is that the majority of the project can be well defined upfront and change should be minimised. These mindsets work well in simple and complicated projects, which is why people rely on them. When you adopt this way of thinking, any change causes frustration and should be avoided.

You can see these standard mindsets at work when you look at any normal project. Most project issues relate to unmet expectations: something wasn't delivered on time or didn't meet the original specification. Take a moment, though, to reflect on the fact that in complexity, the original specification was never going to end up being true or, sometimes, even reasonable. Be alive to the existence of mindsets and understand where people are coming from, recognising that the standard mindsets are ineffective in complexity.

Table 6.1: Standard versus complexity mindsets

STANDARD	COMPLEXITY
Focus on what needs to be delivered Deliver what was asked for	**Keep asking why** Don't start with the answer, let it emerge
Draw on expertise What worked before will work again	**Give up knowing** Look for the brilliance in others
Documents and plans are critical A rigorous, detailed plan is at the heart of project performance	**Always curious** Active inquiry is how you generate insight and drive performance
Control the process Drive out uncertainty	**There is no certainty** Give up on the search for predictability and focus on learning
Detail creates clarity Reduce the problem to its smallest parts to understand it	**Step back, look up** Clarity comes from seeing a bigger picture
Minimise the level of change Minimise change because it makes it hard to deliver the original plan	**Choose your own path** If something isn't working, adjust to match the circumstances

In contrast, the mindsets of the Complex Project Toolkit work with the characteristics of complex projects. For example, focusing on why the project is important rather than what needs to be delivered makes it easier to handle the connected and subjective nature of the situation. Also, being ready and willing to adjust the approach to match the circumstances improves results when the situation is unique and constraints are changing.

This alignment of the mindsets and complexity characteristics, as shown in Figure 6.2, reduces project friction and supports higher performance.

Figure 6.2: Complexity characteristics and mindsets

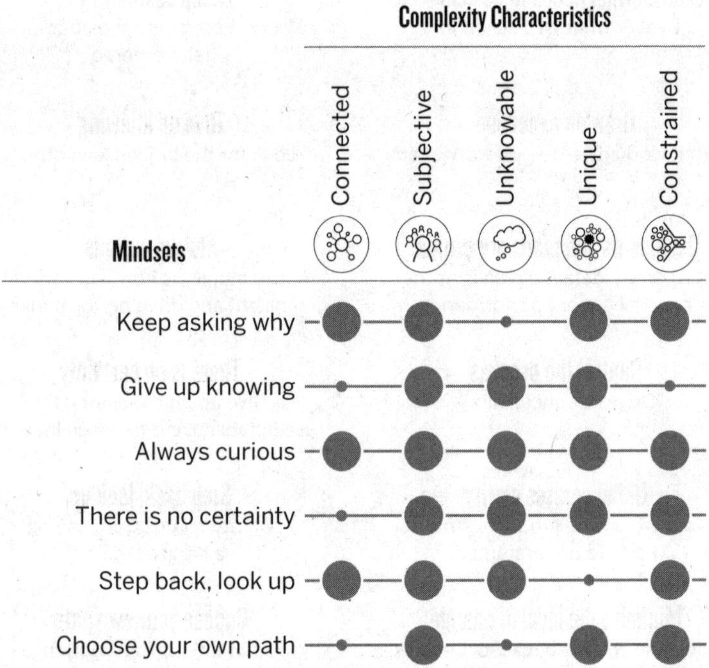

It takes commitment to adopt these mindsets. The challenge is that the existing ways of thinking and behaving are well established and work for normal projects. When I first joined a design firm and saw these mindsets at play, I struggled to work out what was going on. These mindsets come naturally to designers, but for someone with a scientific background like me they just felt wrong. It is a significant shift in thinking, and it's probably going to be uncomfortable, but that's par for the course. That's the journey you are going to have to travel if you take on these new ways of thinking. Chapter 9 contains a discussion of different approaches and challenges when adopting these mindsets as part of the whole Complex Project Toolkit.

What's next?

Now that you are developing a more detailed understanding of the difference between the standard, mechanistic approach and the Complex Project Toolkit, hopefully you are opening up to new possibilities and perhaps frustrated with the current way of working. These new mindsets bring forward possibility and tap into the energy of teams, avoiding the feelings of being trapped and devalued.

In the meantime, keep looking out for the mindsets that are in play in your organisation. Be alive to what the normal mode of operating is and understand where people come from when they hold these mindsets – and recognise how constraining they can be.

This chapter has given you an insight into how complex projects need a new narrative about the nature of project management. The next chapter uses these mindsets as the foundation upon which to build new practices, which are at the heart of the Complex Project Toolkit.

Chapter 7

EFFECTIVE PRACTICES IN COMPLEXITY

'Knowledge is of no value unless you put it into practice.'
—Anton Chekhov

At the core of the Complex Project Toolkit is a set of new practices for project managers. These are effective ways of operating day to day in complex projects and rely on the mindsets introduced in the previous chapter.

The standard project management approach has a set of practices that are well known: define the scope, build a plan, track progress and communicate with stakeholders. They focus on creating certainty and control. They define a way to manage projects – from initiation to planning to execution and completion – that is prescriptive and process-based. The practices of the Complex Project Toolkit are not 'paint-by-number' prescriptive processes; rather, they are guiding heuristics for dealing with complex projects. They represent the missing pieces of the project manager's toolkit that, when used well, reduce frustration and improve the effectiveness of project delivery. A program manager I worked with described these methods as the 'art of project management'.

At the heart of complexity is wickedness – the socially created interpretation of the situation in which no single person has the complete answer. To move forward, you have to recognise there are disparate perspectives and then **connect** them to create a common understanding. Without connections you spend an inordinate amount of energy dealing with issues and misunderstandings. Done well, creating connections reduces the management effort and brings forward new ideas and better ways of working.

But it's not enough to just accumulate a collection of ideas and interpretations across the project. It can add to confusion if left this way, given the shapeshifting nature and overlapping components that are the hallmark of complexity. To operate well, you need to **simplify** the significant issues into a picture or story that provides a guide through the maze of complexity. This makes it easier to see your place in the whole situation and not be overwhelmed by the ambiguity.

Simplifying the situation is rarely straightforward. You need to weigh views against each other, or even generate something completely different. It takes time and requires that you suspend judgement, to **hold space** for new thoughts and insights to arise rather than grab the first answer and go rushing towards the next milestone. This is particularly true when the situation is emergent and only reveals its true nature over time.

Another problem with complexity, where understanding changes as you learn more, is that there is no clear way forward but you still need to deliver results. You have to **find a way** through the ambiguity that is focused on the outcome and unconstrained by current thinking. As the situation changes, you need to probe and push forward, and treat any roadblocks and setbacks as temporary. You can't wait for everything to be in order before you move.

Without a clear plan, and with all the ambiguity and uncertainty and emergence, what keeps you moving forward is the belief that the project is worth doing, that it has a **purpose**. The 'what' and 'how' of the project might evolve, but the 'why' remains constant. Even as the project's scope and approach change, the intent persists. Belief in the purpose of the project will drive you to deliver even when you don't know how, or if, it is possible.

Figure 7.1: Practices of the Complex Project Toolkit

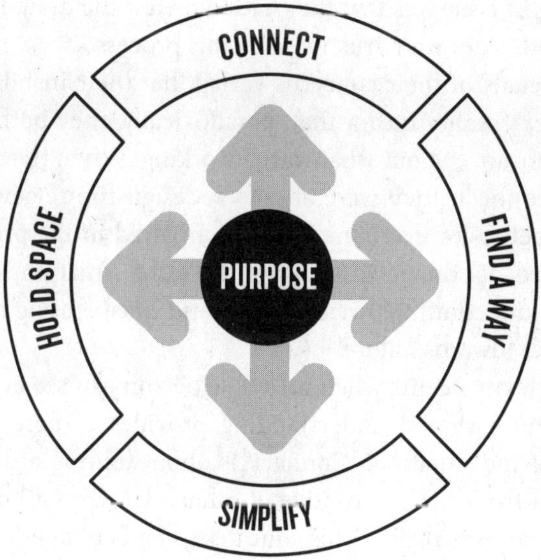

The practices of the Complex Project Toolkit are ways of operating that improve performance and reduce frustration when there is a high degree of ambiguity and uncertainty in the project.

The following sections explore each practice in more detail, providing examples and anecdotes to help you understand the concepts, pitfalls and natural tension that exists between the elements.

Connect

'If you want to go fast, go alone.
If you want to go far, go together.'
—African proverb

When I joined a train design project, the team told me that the final design sign-off was going to miss the deadline by a number of months. Their biggest issue, based on experience with interim submissions, was that the design review by the customer took too long with too many iterations. When talking to the customer, their biggest issue was that they had to review the design so many times. Both sides were frustrated by this process.

The details of their concerns varied, but their inability to see each other's reality meant that, paradoxically, they both had the same annoyance about what wasn't working. When they took the time to connect, they were able to redesign the review process to work better for everyone. If those involved in the project had maintained disconnected views of the same situation, the arguments would continue to be circular and exasperating and drive the project towards failure.

Complexity occurs when no single person can see everything, so creating a shared understanding provides a more complete picture of the situation. 'Connect' is about finding a way to see the world from the perspective of others. It is about being open to someone else's reality. This educates us and enlarges our world. The more we connect with others and their unique perspectives, the easier it is to navigate complexity and improve performance. Connecting requires you to bring together the right people, enhance understanding and generate a collective truth.

'Connect' is about understanding the situation better than you can by yourself through spending time with others in two-way interactions. It can be any type of interaction: a meeting, a workshop, a golf game, a dinner or a company offsite are some examples. The willingness and desire to connect across teams breaks down barriers and makes things happen faster, particularly when there is lots to learn. It's always reciprocal, never one-way.

There are four reasons why connection is important in complex projects:

1. **Understand another's reality:** Only by understanding the experiences of others and connecting world views can we see the whole picture and generate a new truth.
2. **Align around a purpose:** Coming together to define the purpose of a project builds our connection to, and ownership of, the outcome. Shared purpose is unstoppable.
3. **Create context and manage reactions:** Trust plays a crucial role in understanding the nuances of what's going on; standard status reports don't cut it. Connection builds trust and commonality of language.
4. **It's what we do:** We are social beings with a need to relate to others and work with them to create results that are significant and meaningful.

Understand another's reality

When perspectives define reality, failing to understand where others are coming from will leave us constantly frustrated by different interpretations. If you find yourself annoyed by others in a complex situation, ask yourself what opinion they hold that makes their position completely sensible. As Adam Savage from *Mythbusters* said, 'I reject your reality and substitute my own.'

More than just connecting for understanding, this is also about reconciling differences in world views. Time and time again we see diversity in life experience produce much better results than homogenous views or 'individual truth' based on the experiences of one person. You have probably experienced the game at a training event or offsite where, as a team, you are given a scenario – you are in a bushfire, lost in the desert or stuck on a deserted island – with a list of items you need to prioritise. Each person creates their own list, then the group develops a common list. The answers are then compared to the expert ranking. The best group scores are invariably achieved by those who have a strong connection and humility – a willingness to listen and discuss with others.

This is not about creating groupthink, where everyone holds the same view; it is about creating a combined reality that draws from the best bits everyone brings to the table. It is also about knowing your team and being interested in their situation.

Align around a purpose

Have you ever felt the energy that comes from being part of a team with a clear purpose? Whether it is playing in your local soccer team or working for Médecins Sans Frontières, connecting with others around a shared purpose is empowering. It drives us to push through adversity. Connecting over our highest values stands above the complexity. We might disagree about which football team to back, but we can probably agree that we want to make the world better for our children.

I will talk more about purpose and belief later, but fundamentally, purpose provides direction and coordination in the midst of the uncertainty of complexity. Connecting around a purpose is a way to rise above the day-to-day details and ambiguity. In fact, there is a strange symbiotic relationship here: we need to connect to define a shared purpose, but at the same time we use purpose to connect the team.

Create context and manage reactions

The context of any project is created by the environment in which it operates and the people in that ecosystem. The context can change on the whim of individuals. If you are not spending time regularly connecting with stakeholders, then the context will get away from you; it will shift and surprise you as people react in ways you don't expect. Connections allow you both to understand what is going on and also to sense – and, more importantly, to respond to – the emerging situation.

From a practical standpoint, connecting with stakeholders allows you to build trust and manage reactions. All projects will have conflict, but this can be managed more intelligently if you have developed a connection with those involved. It is always harder to criticise or find fault with people you know well.

Complex projects operate across organisational boundaries, either within the organisation or, more commonly, with external parties. Managing the context requires you to connect across organisational boundaries to build trust and increase the ability to get things done when you can't define exactly what you want.

It's what we do

The final reason why connection is important is because being social is part of our biology. As humans, we are fundamentally wired to relate to others, to care for others and to build connections with each other. We are social beings and have a need and a desire to work together on creating things that are meaningful. In the unstable situations of complex projects, connection with other individuals provides the comfort of shared adversity or success. Trouble shared is trouble halved; joy shared is joy doubled.

In his book *Sapiens*, Yuval Noah Harari argues that what sets humans apart from other organisms on the planet is 'the unprecedented ability to cooperate flexibly in large numbers' – not just in rigid patterns like ants, or in small groups like chimpanzees or Neanderthals, but in vast numbers and often with strangers.[1] Only by connecting in meaningful ways around shared stories can we create things that are bigger than ourselves.

Connection is probably more important than most of us realise. Sharing a meal is about more than just the sustenance or having someone else pay (see Box H, overleaf). Research has shown that connection addresses a range of psychological and physical issues, with one study concluding that the opposite of addiction is not abstinence but rather connection with others.[2] Long-term happiness and even longer life spans have been correlated with involvement in the activities of a community.

Doing it well

Connection takes effort to build. It comes through spending time with people in a deliberate and focused way. It requires you to be present in the discussion and not distracted, so you listen intently and pick up on non-verbal signals. If your project is geographically dispersed and relies on remote working, it is worth the time to build connections face-to-face before relying on remote ones.

H: *Sobremesa* – more than just lunch or dinner

Sobremesa is a Spanish word that doesn't translate easily into English. It refers to the time after eating that allows for the settling of food, but more importantly the sharing of ideas and stories, whether true or make-believe. The closest translation might be the 'long lunch'. It celebrates the joy of sharing a meal and the connection that flows from the ensuing conversations – a 2018 *Guardian* article defined it as 'a recognition that there is more to life than working long hours and that few pleasures are greater than sharing a table and then chatting nonsense for a hefty portion of what remains of the day'.[3]

Sharing meals develops strong connections, building empathy and understanding. Research links eating together with a range of health and psychological benefits including reduced obesity, reduced substance abuse and greater tolerance of others when the table is shared with people of diverse backgrounds. The sense of friendship and community created by sharing a meal builds strong bonds and can bring real joy to a situation.

Connection is an evolving process of building 'social credits' with the team members, then using those credits to let you push the boundaries a bit more. Building connection across the team may require building bridges from previous bad experiences. It requires empathy; it requires you to be curious and listen well to understand the other person's reality. The better you know them, the better you can 'speak their language'.

Stories are an effective technique to build connection. Stories contain so much more than just what is said: they provide an insight into where the storyteller is coming from and what is significant to them. The way we interpret the stories and how we relate them to our own experience helps create a connection. Stories help diverse groups with different experiences and views find their point of alignment or areas of common understanding.

Deep connection requires trust, and trust is built through shared experience and common understanding. Special forces training in the military focuses on developing a deep connection and language between team members to generate trust and coordinated action in the most chaotic situations.

Trust is a core element of performing well in complexity. When there is no predictability, trust in each other is all we have to fall back on.

Contention (done well) improves connection

A good team has diversity of experience and thought, so there will be differences of opinion. Contention between team members plays an important role in opening our minds to alternative solutions. Debates that highlight alternative views, when managed effectively, generate new knowledge and team cohesiveness. On one project I worked on, resolving the difference in the expected delivery date between the customer-centric project manager and the product-centric engineering manager increased commitment to the agreed date. It was done in a way that recognised their opinions, connected their world views and amalgamated their realities.

A well-connected team addresses issues early. They don't allow things to fester and grow until they can't be hidden anymore and have a negative impact on progress and morale. Managing contention early builds a discipline for dealing with issues, unloads the issue before it becomes significant and gives the team greater capacity to deal with unknowables.

Worth doing well

Connection, particularly outside the boundaries of organisations, is becoming more and more important and is a key feature of innovation. LEGO connects with customers to vote on which products to launch through their LEGO Ideas program; in 2015 the winner of the Dutch Open Hackathon developed a breakthrough offering that combined services from an airline, airport, bank and department store to deliver presents to arriving or departing passengers at Amsterdam's Schiphol Airport.[4]

Connecting with people is also more effective than directing staff in complexity. It copes with emergence, handles multiple perspectives, opens up new possibilities and generates energy in ambiguity. Connection is not just a vague attempt to 'manage' stakeholders with an occasional update but a genuine desire to define the problem and create the result with those affected. It involves them in the success or failure of the venture. And when they are involved, other benefits flow, including better answers to problems, reduced time and effort to resolve differences, reduced change management effort and more creative environments. Connection improves performance in complexity. On the flipside, how often have you seen an inability or unwillingness to appreciate other points of view lead to frustration and failure?

At the end of the day, you can't demand connection. Connection requires other people to play a part. You have to give up being a technician and open up to those around you. It will take as long as it takes. The skills discussed in Chapter 8 will improve your chances of building effective connections.

Connection will open your eyes to a range of different opinions and approaches. It will broaden what is possible. But to move forward, you need to be able to distil this information into something that is insightful and easily communicated. This is the practice of simplifying.

Simplify

'If you can't explain it simply,
you don't understand it well enough.'
—Albert Einstein

A European military operation had difficulties with a new vehicle acquisition. The project was supposed to use 'off-the-shelf', proven technologies to lower the implementation risk. However, the project was running late and had significant issues that were taking too long to fix. A disproportionate amount of effort was directed towards the growing list of problems. Weekly meetings would go for hours but rarely reach agreement on what actions were required. The most common result was a decision to get more information. When a solution for a particular issue was settled upon, there were further delays because of the detailed justification required to accept the change.

Stepping back and looking at the entire system rather than individual issues, it became clear that the heart of the problem was that the project was customising the vehicle so much that it now looked like a development project rather than the intended off-the-shelf approach. An off-the-shelf project has much lower tolerance for changes and uncertainties, and all the project processes and staffing weren't set up to manage this level of variation.

This simple realisation that this was a development project encapsulated and explained the majority of problems – delays in delivery of components, invoices not matching the original contract, increased testing regimes and timeframes, to name a few. It also explained why the customer and the supplier could never come to an agreement in the meetings.

This understanding shifted the project approach towards managing it as a research project, which profoundly changed the nature of the interaction with the supplier, allowing a greater tolerance for adjustments and rework. Prior to this, variability and uncertainty were a constant source of irritation. The revised classification of the project fundamentally shifted the level of frustration, the alignment between all the stakeholders and the chance of successful delivery.

This is what simplifying is about – finding the clear, concise and compelling object (in this case, the revised naming of the project as a development project) that cuts through the messiness and focuses on the things that matter. Where connection seeks out more and more information and perspectives, simplifying brings everything back to the key points, the 'killer slide' or the message that just makes sense. This makes it easier to interact with the emergent and shapeshifting nature of complexity, to coordinate effort and drive effective action.

Simplifying is not a concept within the standard project management approach. Project managers look to pull apart the project deliverables into smaller, more manageable components and then build a work breakdown structure that provides specific, detailed activities that can be handed out to the team members. Simplifying does the opposite. It looks 'up and out' rather than 'down and in', because a reductionist approach to complexity creates confusion. It looks across the environment for a simple description that gets to the heart of the matter.

Simplifying is the most creative of all the practices in the toolkit and is difficult to prescribe and time-box. It is an iterative process in which you make time to *understand* the whole situation, *synthesise* a model that brings forward the significant themes and *review* the power of the model to explain what is going on (see Figure 7.2). It is not a simplistic grouping of topics into a few categories or lists of ideas. Doing it well takes time and energy.

Figure 7.2: Actions to simplify

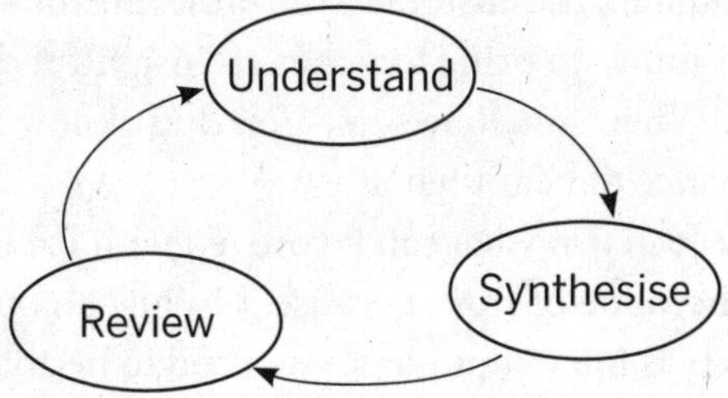

The act of making a model and debating it with others creates questions, drives greater understanding and further refines the model. This cycle continues until the model – a diagram, a metaphor, a naming of the situation, or whatever works – is cohesive and provides insights that cut through the uncertainty and make it easier to operate in complexity.

Understand

To be able to simplify, you need to comprehend the nuances of the project; you should spend the majority of your time and effort developing a deep understanding of the situation. It's about searching widely to understand the context of the situation and then diving beneath the initial stories and 'mythbusting' to get to the detailed layers below. Designers refer to this phase of the journey as 'exploration and discovery'.

Understanding does come from data, and this is often the first place we go to because it can provide a strong basis for a discussion. However, stories can provide more nuanced insights than numbers. As Jeff Bezos from Amazon once put it, '…the thing I have noticed is that when the anecdotes and the data disagree, the anecdotes are usually right.'[5]

Stories allow us to add our own interpretation and colour to the situation. They make it easier to empathise with those involved, particularly when strong differences of opinion get in the way of listening. The willingness to understand the experience of others – the builder, the customer, the project team – significantly increases our ability to bring together an insightful description of the situation. When someone says, 'You don't know what it's like,' that's your chance to hear their story.

A singular focus on what can be proven with data can lead you to discount the value of story because it is 'just an opinion'. Given that complexity is full of opinions, you need to be able to interpret the data and, more importantly, look for resonance in the stories. The real art in complexity is to distinguish between the stories that are useful and those which are distracting.

Convenient stories and mistruths

When I first joined an aircraft build project that was underway, I would often hear that the aircraft was no good because it couldn't fly at night. I heard this story so often that it sounded like some really weird physics was going on; I had impressions of the aircraft losing power as the sun set. It turns out that it wasn't that it was incapable of flying at night, just that the government regulator didn't allow it to operate at night. Digging further into why, it turned out that the anti-collision lights (the red flashing beacons you see on aircraft) were in the wrong place. They were in the wrong place because the aircraft had been developed for a different jurisdiction with different requirements.

The problem was solved by repositioning the beacons. But the detractors of the project loved the story that the brand-new, highly sophisticated aircraft couldn't fly at night. The story was 'true', but the interpretation was false, or at least being used disingenuously. Urban Dictionary defines these as 'mistruths' – statements that are true but misleading. Whenever you come across one of these, it probably gives you more insight into the social nature of the situation (in this case, the negativity of the project team) than the topic of the story (the aircraft's performance).

In complexity, be careful of taking things at face value, or blindly applying information without knowing the context. Be curious. Simplistic answers are very appealing; they make us feel smart quickly. They give us a sense that we have understanding in what is often a time-pressured and foggy situation. It is not unusual for team members to grasp at any scrap of information to make themselves appear knowledgeable. Don't be a 'lazy expert' who quotes, or even misquotes, what others have said without doing the work to understand the context and reality.

Ambiguity seems to breed this type of response within normally sensible people. I'm sure you've experienced times when a person grabs a snippet of information – an anecdote, a detailed figure or similar – in order to appear expert, only for you to find out later that the source was misinterpreted or misrepresented. Napoleon wasn't shorter than average, the Great Wall of China is not the only man-made object visible from space, you don't have to wait 30 minutes after eating to go for a swim and bulls don't hate the colour red.

Beware of misguided anecdotes or rhetorical fallacies which appear sensible at first glance but lack strong logic and are designed to manipulate your understanding of what is true.[6] In *The Demon-Haunted World*, Carl Sagan writes that people are 'unable to distinguish between what feels good and what's true'. He describes the 'celebration of ignorance' that has meant that well-supported scientific theories carry the same or less weight than explanations made up on the spot by 'authorities' whom people have lost the ability to 'knowledgeably question'.[7] Often, we don't have patience for complexity, but it is important to sit with the problem and push understanding further by asking lots of questions.

Lots of things are unknowable, but that doesn't mean you should be complacent. You need to go into detail to get beyond a simplistic statement. Go down five levels to reveal the inherent complexity of the system. Many of the detailed elements, such as underlying assumptions and connections, are hidden from view.

These need to be understood if you are going to find a powerful simplification of the situation.

Understanding is about developing a nuanced picture of the situation. Somewhere between the simplistic view you first walk in with and the 'if you haven't worked here for 30 years' position lies some valuable information. It comes from the conversations, the interactions, the stories and the data as they coalesce to provide insight into the way things are and why. It is the first step on the way to simplifying the complexity.

Synthesise

Taking the time to understand can result in a cluster of apparently disconnected ideas. You can't just leave it as a series of disparate stories and data points; it is too hard to interact with the system in this state. Once you comprehend the details of the situation, you need to develop a structure – a model, a drawing, a story or even a new naming of the situation – that cuts through the complexity.

Rarely is an insightful model obvious; it takes time and effort. In complexity it helps to look at the problem from a range of different angles or frames of reference. Reframing the situation is aided by stories and metaphors that expose embedded assumptions, encouraging you to step beyond your existing thoughts and biases to explore alternative models.

Reframing brings forward new insights and ways of thinking. However, it is not just about picking one idea and running with it. At some point all these ideas need to be synthesised into a coherent model that cuts through the complexity.

Within all the immersion and research and conversations, there is a point – a flash of insight and creativity – where all the information is brought together with the right people at the right time. As Jon Kolko, the founder of the Austin Center for Design, describes it, 'there continues to appear something magical about synthesis when encountered in professional practice... Synthesis reveals a cohesion and sense of continuity; synthesis indicates a push towards organization, reduction, and clarity.'[8]

Synthesis is solidly within the realm of designers and strategists. They are famous for the brilliance that occurs in the synthesis of new insights from seemingly chaotic mounds of research and data and stories. They call it 'sense-making'.

It is about looking for patterns, which is something humans are much better at doing than computers in the social messiness of complexity. It is a search for significance – a search for those elements that will have the most impact on the outcomes or constraints. It is a balancing act of what to keep and what to leave out. Technicians can struggle with this search for significance because they see every part of the system as equally important – nothing can be left out – and there isn't a clear process to follow.

The skills associated with doing this well are covered in the next chapter.

Review

The model you develop to simplify the situation has to be socialised to ensure it makes sense to others. There is no point having a model that needs to be constantly explained – it only adds to the complexity.

It is easy to get caught in the trap of pushing towards confirming the first idea you come up with. Confirmation bias – our desire to ratify what we already believe and keep doing what we are doing – is strong, particularly under time pressure, and will constrain our ability to see alternative options.

Genuine insight and simplification requires you to be open to alternative views, to test what has been developed and be willing to adjust perspective as you learn. The best way to do this is to treat your model as your current point of view that can be changed (see Box I, overleaf). Put it up for review and see if it survives. Try to break it. Be curious and willing to learn.

I: Using a point of view

'The difficulty lies, not in the new ideas,
but in escaping from the old ones.'
—John Maynard Keynes

A point of view is your current answer. Calling it a 'point of view' indicates it can change – it represents the existing thinking but not necessarily the final thinking. The intent is to use it to validate how you see the world. Sometimes you hold it in your back pocket and listen to what is going on, always considering how the things you see and hear impact upon it. Other times you put it on the table for all to see and pass comment on.

The importance of using this approach correctly was brought home to me on a project with an insurance firm. We were developing a new car insurance process and had set up a workroom where people could come and review the design to date, add their comments and contribute any insights they might have. The room represented our current point of view about how things could operate.

After a week I visited the room, and something looked wrong. It was formatted nicely, showing clear paths through the process. But it lacked the usual messiness of Post-it notes and scribbles I would expect. I soon found out that the consultant running the sessions would get people into the room and walk them through the process and explain how things would be done. He wouldn't cover any topic until it had been drawn up nicely. If anyone disagreed, he would argue why his point of view made sense. He wasn't listening for their comments. He wasn't trying to find the flaws in the system. He was trying to prove he had got it right. This is not how you use a point of view in complexity; it was exactly the opposite of what we were trying to do.

When you use a point of view, you can't be concerned about the look of what you make. You have to put an object out there even if it isn't well formed. Look for passion and what gets a reaction from those in the room. Contention is to be encouraged, not feared.

Reviewing your model with others can identify gaps, but it can also cause delays when everyone wants to add their insight. You can be dragged down the path of the particular pet ideas of people who get involved. It is also possible to end up in infinite loops or circular arguments. I've often encountered the problem where you build a picture – say, a functional view of an organisation – and the feedback is that it lacks the nuances of the various locations of the business. So, you build a geographic view, which then lacks the nuances of functional view. And the circular debates begin.

The ideal simplification creates a reaction, a 'light-bulb' moment or realisation. It highlights something that has been hidden – it might be assumptions, or gaps, or some kind of incongruence in the current activities – and brings it to life. It creates clarity and galvanises action in a way that might not have been considered before. The example from the beginning of this section, where the military project turned out to be a research and development project and not 'off the shelf', is an example of a simple naming that drove a significant improvement.

Recognise that simplifying is a creative process, and at some point you have to make a call and accept any imperfections. Take the feedback, pick the model that has the most power over the situation and move on.

Worth doing well

Projects' status reports come in a range of formats and styles. They can be text-heavy or full of graphics. Unfortunately, most reports become a plate on which to serve up as much information as possible rather than answering the real question at hand. I saw one report that gave the client detailed information about the timing of activities and resource usage across the project, but it was unreadable. The numbers were accurate, but the form of the presentation made it extremely difficult to understand where things were at. When the status report was simplified to focus on the items that were significant, the chief executive said it was the first time he felt he was not being lied to. Simplification not only made it easier to manage the project, it also built trust.

The practice of simplifying cuts through the complexity to reduce cognitive load. An effective simplification abstracts the details and allows you to see the whole situation at once. It is an overall map of the territory that makes it easier to interact with the complexity.

The act of simplifying the situation guides and constrains the actions you take. It helps you avoid distractions and focus on the few things that matter. So, how do you know when you have it right? That's a judgement call that is more art than science, but it often comes with the realisation that you have found a better way to understand the whole situation.

What stands in the way

Simplifying is about creating the naming that cuts through complexity, and this takes time. Standard project management focuses on time as a key constraint. If there is a question to be answered, it is ideally answered as soon as possible. In contrast, simplifying requires you to engage in dialogue and follow paths of discovery. Project managers in complex projects need to resist the rush to lock in the first answer and move on. The implications of moving quickly with an ineffective picture won't be realised for weeks, months or even years. Be willing to take the time to do it well.

Three things stand in the way of doing this practice well:

1. **Time pressure:** Time-boxing undermines genuine exploration and synthesis. Time constraints are real, so keep things moving – but don't shut down valuable discussions because of the clock. Be willing to extend discussions or come back to things to understand the nuances and stories. One of the biggest dangers in developing understanding in ambiguous situations is the push for an answer to fit the schedule. This leads you to not engage in a dialogue, not listen

to what is coming up in the discussion and potentially miss crucial details that will surprise you later.

2. **Shutting down idea branches:** This is about allowing time but not letting the discussion run in directions that aren't immediately obvious. Give yourself the space to wander into ideas that at first glance don't look to you like they will be productive. It might be that others interpret the same situation differently. Let the discussion run.
3. **A closed mind:** Simplification needs divergence and convergence. Bring your curiosity and hold your own point of vicw lightly. Be curious, explore and learn rather than trying to confirm a preconceived idea. Evolution requires mutation and death. Let your ideas be murdered by better ones.

Simplicity lies on the other side of complexity. I don't remember who first told me that, but I've found it has always held up. This practice of simplifying creates a clear, concise and compelling naming, image or story that places everything in context. But it takes time and effort. It requires a willingness to sit with the problem, reframe it with powerful metaphors and stories, and distil themes from a deep understanding. All of this takes time – time to explore, time to understand, time to reflect – which on the surface it might seem like you don't have in a project. This leads to the next practice of the Complex Project Toolkit: the ability to hold space to create the time to think.

Hold space

'To discern what is truly essential we need space to think, time to look and listen, permission to play, wisdom to sleep...'
—Greg McKeown, *Essentialism*[9]

The Manhattan Project developed the nuclear bomb for the Allies during World War II. The project brought together some of the leading scientists from around the world, such as Niels Bohr, Hans Bethe, Enrico Fermi and Richard Feynman, who have all received the Nobel Prize in Physics. The scientists were working at the cutting edge of what was known at the time, with materials only recently discovered and techniques that only existed in theory. They had to develop new models to explain what would happen and new tools to construct what was required.

Robert Oppenheimer, a theoretical physicist from the University of California, Berkeley, was the head of the Los Alamos National Laboratory, which led the research. The project ran at a frenetic pace because, in the context of the wars in Europe and the Pacific, whoever tamed the atom first would set the world order. Even within this pressured environment, Oppenheimer would gather his team together each Friday, interrupting their demanding and critical research, for a colloquium to bring disparate ideas together and 'encourage new ideas', because he realised 'each one must know the whole thing if he was to be creative'.[10]

Holding space is about taking the time to reflect, think, consider and suspend judgement – to bring forward different points of view and allow alternative realities to emerge. It is fundamentally about taking the time to learn. A bias for learning is a prerequisite for performing well in complexity, given the level of unknowables and emergence. This practice delays locking in the answer while you actively explore options. A good answer emerges from a diversity of points of view, and these take time to gather and process.

One of the most significant ways design thinking differs from standard, reductionist thinking is in the use of divergence – exploring alternative options, different opinions and higher levels of the system you are operating in. Exploration is not about searching for confirmation of your belief, but rather about curiously wandering through the topic while keeping an open mind. It takes a willingness to suspend your point of view, to assume you don't have the answer and to question the world, as discussed in the last section. Convergence back to the answer also takes time for synthesising and simplifying. All of this requires you to create the space for this learning and thinking to occur.

Crossing the uncertainty gap

One of the strongest desires in complexity is to remove the uncertainty. The faster you name and tame a wicked situation, the faster you remove the uncertainty and push forward with an answer. However, without taking the time for discovery and exploration, this early taming limits the answer to whatever is in front of you at the time. Taming early might feel like progress, but as you gather more information, the original answer will change and, as discussed in Chapter 3, decisions that are made without a global view get revisited, throwing the plan into chaos. In complexity, we have to resist the temptation to name and tame quickly.

Holding space isn't just about slowing everything down; it is about crossing the uncertainty gap in a deliberate and effective way. The common mistake is to bridge the gap with a defined position that you are trying to prove, rather than using a methodical approach to build understanding. To resist locking in your first answer requires a comfort with ambiguity (see Box J, over the page). You can't hold space if you are in a rush to get past the ambiguity and into certainty. Additionally, if you don't see the need to take time to reflect and learn, then the implication is that the design is as good as it can be.

Holding space is about doing the work to make sure decisions with high impact, that commit effort to a particular direction, are well thought through. Actively use the space to progress understanding until it is good enough to move forward. It takes time, effort and judgement, and is an art rather than a science. The challenge is to develop a point of view as early as possible but lock it in as late as possible.

J: Levels of comfort with ambiguity

It is important that the project team is able to suspend judgement and hold space while they consider alternatives. Team members need to be okay with operating in ambiguity, where they don't know the answer and are willing to let it emerge over time.

But not everyone is the same. When it comes to comfort with ambiguity, there are four types of people:

1. **Don't see it:** They are blissfully ignorant that the situation is complex and are not in a rush to close it out, because they don't see it as a problem of any significance. They are in a happy place, but when you point out the ambiguity they can quickly become the next type of person...
2. **See it and are bothered by it:** They are overwhelmed by the ambiguity and want the pain to stop. Because of the cognitive dissonance caused by the lack of knowing, they will rush to find an answer to the situation. In my experience, this represents the majority of the project population and is where most of a project manager's time and effort is directed.
3. **Okay with it:** They see the ambiguity and know it is a problem but are comfortable for it to continue for a while, although not for too long. They have identified the ambiguity as a problem, something to be addressed at some stage, but they can hold their breath long enough to get through it. More and more people identify with this perspective as the level of complexity in workplaces has risen.
4. **It just is:** Whereas the previous group see ambiguity as a problem to be outlasted, this group accept it as a fact of life. They don't consider ambiguity good or bad – at any moment, it just is. This group is most able to operate well when holding space because their cognitive process is not compromised by the uncertainty.

The higher the level of comfort with ambiguity in the team, the easier it is to create the space and consider alternatives without rushing to tame the situation too quickly.

Taking time to think

In complex projects, time to think and reflect is always difficult to find, but you have to make that time. A mentor of mine was fond of the maxim 'quality of thought creates economy of motion'. Making time to think in complex projects is valuable because your understanding of the situation is constantly evolving. You need to continually check whether your model of the world still holds true or if something has come up that compels you to change your point of view.

To achieve this, you need to hold space at two levels. The first is within the team. This requires you to ensure team members don't jump to conclusions and that they recognise that any answer only reflects the current thinking and could change. This can be difficult in technical organisations where individuals can see answers as absolute. Holding space is a critical element of using the 'point of view' technique described in Box I (page 140). You also need to lead the team so that they maintain the humility and openness to contemplate alternative and potentially better solutions.

The second level of this practice is within the broader environment of the project. A critical role of the project manager is to influence the external context. In complexity, their role is to keep the 'barbarians from the gate', so the team have the time and opportunity to explore and evaluate options. When things are unclear there will be pressure from outside the team to provide answers and to tame the problem quickly. In complex projects, given that perspectives define reality, you can alter constraints and shift priorities by adjusting perceptions and interpretations of the situation. Creating the right context is a key skill for delivering complex projects.

Creating space

Holding space requires discipline, not only in creating the time and willingness to share ideas, but also in being willing to do what appears to be nothing. Don't underestimate the value of boredom.

Don't try filling every moment with the 'planet's worth of entertainment in your pocket' (as a 2017 *Wired* article put it[11]), but rather allow yourself to drift into a state of greater thoughtfulness. Making space to reflect is at the core of creativity, insights and realising what is important. As I mentioned in Chapter 6, a simple technique is to take some time to sit with a blank sheet of paper to see what ideas emerge.

It is not about sitting around on cushions, staring at whiteboards while cogitating about the world. It is about deliberately making time to think and learn. 'Nothing is harder to do these days than nothing... in a world where our value is determined by our 24/7 data productivity ... doing nothing may be our most important form of resistance.' So argues artist and critic Jenny Odell.[12] Odell sees our attention as the most precious resource we have. Once we can start paying a new kind of attention, she suggests, we can undertake bolder forms of action, reimagine humankind's role in the environment, and arrive at more meaningful understandings of happiness and progress. In complex projects, this time to think can bring forward a clarity about the way forward, either at the level of the entire system or even just today's tasks.

Designers are able to suspend their judgement very well. For those of us with a scientific or management background, holding space can feel like wasting time. The answer is obvious to us, particularly when we have relevant experience, so why not just lock it in and move on? However, if you accept that in complexity, perspectives define reality and the situation is unique, you understand that you'll rarely get the best answer the first time.

It can be hard to have the patience to work towards something better. A friend of mine had a low golf handicap, but he wanted it to be low single digit. The golf professional said that to get lower, he had to unlearn a few things. He would teach him new techniques, but his handicap would get worse before it got better. If he didn't suspend his judgement he would never cross the gap. The benefit of suspending judgement can take time to reveal itself.

He also had to cope with the critical comments of others as he made the transition.

Worth doing well

One of the significant differences between normal operations and projects is that revisiting decisions on projects is very expensive. Imagine trying to change the concrete foundations of a building after you have already constructed a few levels. I have seen effective operational managers fail in projects because they make quick decisions, as you need to in operational environments, without taking the time to understand the longer-run implications.

Without creating the space and time to reflect, particularly when the situation is emergent, you will miss the signals that guide how you should react and which parts need your attention.

A number of things stand in the way of holding space:

- **Time pressure:** As with Simplify, the urgency to get things done is the biggest killer of the ability to hold space. The desire to just move forward with what you have is very strong. There will always be a logic for moving quickly, but it is important to remember that you don't want to have to revisit decisions because significant insights were left out.
- **Permission to keep looking:** While not necessarily overtly stated, permission is needed to take time to consider alternatives when you already have a potential answer.
- **Discomfort with ambiguity:** To do this well you need to be okay with both not knowing and also with having an answer but suspending judgement while looking for a better one. Pulling this off in a fast-paced world takes considerable self-confidence.
- **How much is enough?** It is always hard – indeed it is an art – to tell if you have spent enough time on a topic, which means the time is often cut short.

It can't go on forever

Holding space is about swapping the appearance of certainty for the confidence of delivery. It is about holding off 'pouring the concrete' around your ideas until they are well informed.

However, it can't go on indefinitely. At some point you have to lock in the ideas, pick an answer and move forward – that is the fundamental nature of a project. The real art is finding the balance and knowing when you have spent enough time on a topic. This takes judgement and experience, because at some point you do need to keep moving and find a way to deliver.

Find a way

'When going through hell, don't stop.'
—Anon.

In complex projects, where information is contingent on events that haven't happened yet, you often find yourself in a situation you weren't expecting, out of time and with no clear sense of how to get to the end. The common reaction, when coming from a traditional project management approach, is to reduce the scope to create clarity or extend the timeframe. This is driven by the belief in the fixed nature of the trade-offs between time, cost and scope – project management's 'golden triangle'.

Finding a way is about always looking for a way to achieve the result regardless of the situation that presents itself. This is not about throwing out planning, or ignoring promises about timelines and outcomes. It is about being relentless and unstoppable – in reviewing options, questioning constraints and redesigning the approach to deliver on the intent despite the uncertainties and challenges thrown at you. It is about not being constrained by standard project management thinking (see Box K).

Complexity requires the ability and willingness to sense and respond to emergence. If you hold fast to static plans and status

K: Shift the triangle

Much has been written about the 'golden triangle' – the idea that cost, time and quality are all connected, and that improving one has to be detrimental to one or both of the others. For example, if you want faster delivery, then the cost will go up or quality will suffer. But the underlying assumption is that you are maintaining the same approach.

Rethinking the approach can 'shift the triangle', driving improvement on all dimensions, in a similar way that new technology fundamentally reshapes the productivity in, and economics of, an industry.

An example of this is the reshaping of the review process of a train design that I discussed in the previous chapter. The original approach was to submit documents for review, get feedback, update the documents, resubmit them for review, and continue until no more comments were made. Each step took two to three weeks. Rethinking the approach to start with a two-day collaborative walk-through of the design, make adjustments during the sessions and then submit the revised document for review resulted in a significant reduction in both review time and cost, and increased accuracy.

Rethinking the approach doesn't always have to be as significant as a program redesign. It can be as simple as an event that brings people together and pushes everyone to resolve the last few percent of a problem before they have to put it on show.

Shifting the triangle takes a willingness to be unconstrained and unreasonable. Every time I've managed to rethink an approach, there was always at least one person who said it couldn't be done that way.

However, there also have to be sensible limits on how creative you get. The Voskhod program of the Soviet Union was the first to put three people into space at once. They did this by stripping out the interior of the Vostok capsule designed for one cosmonaut. They removed the ejection seat and conditions were so cramped the occupants couldn't wear space suits.[13] Kudos for creativity, and they all came back alive, but it was high risk. Less extreme was the time a project manager used developers to do the User Acceptance Testing because it would be 'significantly faster'; this is not the way to do it. Rethink the approach, focus on the outcome, but don't skip critical elements.

reports when the situation is unknown and unique, your project will be in trouble in no time at all. If you stay on the original path as the world changes and information points you in a different direction, you will overwork your team on useless activities and hasten the demise of the project.

Finding a way still draws on the design thinking model but moves towards project-focused disciplines. Designers are great at creating something new, but they normally don't have the temperament for the painful process of getting things done in complexity. Projects are hard and often full of zero-sum trade-offs in highly constrained and political, sometimes even threatening, environments. A group of designers I worked with on a project described the environment as 'aggressive, argumentative, unpleasant and confronting to work in.'[14]

While this practice draws on design thinking by anchoring the outcome and solving for the constraints that are real, this practice relies on urgency to relentlessly work the problem and not be distracted by the challenging environments that exist in projects.

Anchor the outcome

Start with the outcome in mind and work back to what is required to make it happen. This might seem obvious, but this is often lacking. As you adjust your approach to changing conditions, keep asking: does this move me closer or further away from the intent of the project? Having clarity about the outcome lifts you above the day-to-day noise and distractions. Clarity about why you are doing the project rather than what is being delivered cuts through the complexity and underpins the ability to do 'right-to-left planning', as discussed in the next chapter.

Following Hurricane Katrina in 2005, New Orleans faced a large and growing homelessness problem. In 2007 the city put together a targeted program to bring that number down by 90%. Martha Kegel, executive director of UNITY of Greater New Orleans, described a three-pronged approach. First was putting together an outreach team that 'was willing to go anywhere and do anything to rescue and rehouse a homeless person'. Second was to put effort behind building a rehousing fund, and third was to accept people as they were, whatever state they were in.

Driving all of this was a strongly stated belief: 'We have to provide housing for people with disabilities. We have to have housing for the elderly. We have to make sure that children aren't homeless. That's part of being a healthy community and a country that has a moral core.'[15] They delivered without a detailed plan or scope; they just knew the outcome and three things to focus on.

Solve for the constraint

The lack of clarity in complexity can cause confusion when responding to changes as they emerge. Focus has to be given to the actions that address the most significant constraints, because these will have the biggest impact on achieving the outcome.

When I joined one project, it was running behind schedule, and the delivery estimate was that it would be at least 12 months away if everything went well. The project was consuming millions of dollars a month, and a delay of this size was unacceptable. We had to find a way to reduce the duration of the project.

Going through the detail of the project, it became clear that the test development, execution and review process was the critical path for completion. The existing design of the process meant there was no way of knowing how many iterations would occur, which added significant uncertainty to the delivery dates.

We redesigned the test process to reduce the time required. Time-saving became the mantra, and every element was reviewed. New tools were purchased, better information flows were established and additional expertise was added. Additional funding was required to support the process, but this was a small price compared to the run rate of the project and the value of the milestone payment. We found a way and the milestone was delivered on time.

Solving for the constraint means that the approach is designed around the critical feature of the project. If time is of the essence, then redesign the elements that consume the most time. If resources are the constraint, then work to unload them or reduce the reliance on their involvement, always with a focus on the outcome.

Given the criticality of the constraints, report progress against them. If stakeholder agreement is critical, then design your approach around this and measure how it is improving. How often have you seen consultations with stakeholders arranged in a way that is more about going through the motions rather than achieving agreement, with progress reported as the number of meetings held? If you are just reporting the number of activities undertaken, don't expect progress against the constraint.

Relentlessly work the problem

Finding a way means you are not going to just stay the current course. Your overall disposition needs to be discomfort with the current approach, questioning the status quo and always looking for a better way. You need to be willing to step back and question what has gone before, and be unreasonable in your requests. If the problem is important enough, get the best people in a room for a solid week and rethink the project approach to find an effective response. Fresh minds can also bring new energy and perspectives. It is easier to be unreasonable when facing a major disruption or issue.

The alternative to finding a way is to accept the situation and stick to the plan. In doing this, you also accept underperformance on the project. Even if there are real limitations, you don't have to be passive. Comments such as 'It is what it is' and 'There is nothing I can do' get in the way. These reflect someone being a victim to the environment rather than crafting the situation to be what it needs to be. It is about constantly pushing for a better way, regardless of the obstacles.

Worth doing well

This practice, done well, increases the energy in the project. It is impossible to be passive and execute on this practice. It requires you to sense and respond, check your assumptions and adjust, and keep moving. Performing this practice well requires three disciplines:

1. **Don't wait for certainty:** I worked with a business to redesign the structure of their maintenance operation. We co-created three designs that included five new roles, and selected a preferred option. However, the decision was delayed three months while a detailed risk review was conducted. The reality was that it would have been relatively easy to swap between the three designs down the track if the analysis highlighted any issue. In complexity, it is easy to let the unknowns be an excuse for delaying delivery until there is more clarity and information. Recognise this possibility and press on, knowing you have to make a decision in the middle of the uncertainty.
2. **Manage the context:** This practice is not just about moving quickly; it needs to be done in a coordinated way that deliberately moves things forward. There is a danger of leaving stakeholders behind in a 'sense and respond' approach. Keeping stakeholders up to date is essential to survive and prosper, otherwise the context can get away from you. You have to educate the executives to accept this mode of interaction. When adjusting approaches, there is a greater need to keep stakeholders updated, because if they feel uninformed or out of control they can wreck your day.
3. **Keep learning:** When adjusting the approach in complexity, you need to be attuned to what has improved and what has degraded. As discussed previously, with wicked problems the situation will change with every action that is taken, and there is no way of knowing the full impact before taking action.

Complex projects are emergent, and the path from the beginning to the end is never clear. A fundamental practice for operating well in complexity is the willingness to question your approach and make changes as required. If you are focused on maintaining the original plan, then, as the world reveals itself as being different from your original conception, you will waste energy and time. You will pursue activities and priorities that no longer move you towards the real outcome.

To really find a way, you need to be fearless. You need to be comfortable with messiness because you don't have three days to polish your ideas. You need to be willing to iterate quickly, to move when uncertain, to find out what does and doesn't work. You need to maintain a relentless pace and not be worried about rejection and judgement. You need to make calls and own the result, which is made easier when you believe you are doing something worthwhile.

Purpose

> *'If you want to build a ship, don't drum up the men and women to gather wood, divide the work, and give orders. Instead, teach them to yearn for the vast and endless sea.'*
>
> —Antoine de Saint-Exupéry

A 2017 study by neuroscientist Tara Swart found that journalists drank more alcohol and less water than recommended and had a diet high in sugar. Their hours were abnormally irregular, their pay low and they faced constant deadlines. They showed the effects of poor sleep and bad nutrition. Many of the study's participants said they had no time for breaks while working. Despite all of this, the journalists showed a better-than-average ability to cope and were no more physically stressed than the average person.

The report found that 'the meaning and purpose they attribute to their work contributes to helping them remain mentally resilient'.[16] The journalists' belief in what they were doing made it easier for them to cope with the stress and uncertainty of their position. This is not a standalone result. Other research has shown that people who believe their job serves a noble goal are more productive and are willing to perform it for less money.[17]

Transcending complexity

Belief in a higher-order purpose transcends complexity. It focuses your mind and energy. It is the 'why' that underpins the 'what' and drives you to find a 'how'. It is the reason for pushing on even when others might give up or implore you to stop. It is the basis of what drives you to achieve, even when you don't know details.

When the engineering manager on a project that was off the rails saw there was renewed support for achieving the goal, he told me, 'I don't know how to get there, but I will sweat blood trying to make it happen.' This was not about objectives. It was not about the plan. It was about his will to make it happen. At times, he was the only person who believed it was possible. Purpose doesn't come from analysis; it is something you craft and own.

It's personal

Meaning. Purpose. Will. Ambition. Belief. Desire. Passion. All potential titles for this section. It was never going to be 'Objective' or 'Outcome', because these are cold representations of a situation and can be detached from the individual. Purpose is personal – it is about creating something that is important to you. It is not something you have been asked to do. You do it because you want to, because it is worthy of your time, energy and love. The meaning that you attribute to the project has an edge that cuts through complexity and makes it both possible and worthwhile to succeed. This personal attachment is essential if you want to push through complexity and triumph despite your desire for certainty.

When you believe in what you are doing, it is so much harder to back down. One of the real risks in complex projects, particularly when things are not going well and the surprises are increasing, is that people will give up. Giving up could involve allowing the deadline to slip or the functionality to be less than intended. A strong purpose will drive you to resist this.

Purpose drives pace

Following the 1996 Port Arthur massacre in Australia, in which 35 people lost their lives, representatives from all legal and political jurisdictions put aside their differences to push through national gun-control legislation in record time. They were not slowed by the technical complexities of rim-fire versus centre-fire guns, magazine sizes, or uncertainties about the impact on farmers, collectors and sporting shooters. They were not deterred by the counterarguments. They believed in the need to make guns less accessible and in two days were able to sort out the details underpinning the new laws, which most thought would take months. They saw a context that was so much bigger than any individual or organisation or factional interest. They all saw meaning and importance in their work and had the will to get this done quickly to stop such senseless violence happening again.

If you have ever had to push through a contentious decision, you know the importance of will. Even when you can't prove your path, or when there are naysayers, it is the will to get it done that drives you forward.

Belief fills the gaps

Assumptions are at the heart of complexity because of the inability to draw on previous experience. In the absence of proof or previous experience, all assumptions are based on what you believe to be true.

When developing a new labour agreement for a new maintenance operation, one of the sticking points was the amount of sick leave available to staff. One group of managers argued that increasing the allowed sick leave limit would undermine productivity because the staff would take more leave, as they had in other parts of the business. Another group argued that while that might be true elsewhere, this unit had a fundamentally different culture. They believed the increased limit would not lead to an escalation in absences and would be a goodwill gesture that would get the agreement signed. Neither side could prove their prediction of the future. In complexity, you get to choose the assumptions based on what you believe to be true and your intent for the situation.

If things are true or false according to what you believe, then pick a belief that lifts people up. Daniel DeNicola, chair of philosophy at Gettysburg College in Pennsylvania, said (while talking about the impact one person's beliefs can have on others) that 'one's "will to believe" entitles us to choose to believe the alternative that projects a better life'.[18]

Purpose creates meaning

Meaning is something we, as humans, add to everything. We get to decide if something is meaningful. Often just achieving the challenge, solving the problem or doing something that others thought could not be done is meaning enough. Sometimes you need to look to a much wider context, however, to find a positive meaning in a difficult and complex project.

In 2013, the Australian airline Qantas was facing amplified competition and recorded a loss of $2.7 billion, the largest in its history. In response, a transformation program involved the loss of 5000 jobs, about 15% of the workforce. What is the purpose of this reduction? Do you believe this was justified? Should they have worked harder to save the jobs? What meaning do you put on this reduction?

It is very hard to see cost reduction as having a good purpose, but I would argue that even the torturous process of significant cost reduction and transformation can invoke pride in the long run if you believe it is necessary. By way of contrast, Thomas Cook Group, Britain's largest travel agency, went into liquidation in September 2019 after being in business for 178 years. Could a large and painful transformation have helped save that business? Do you believe it would have been worth the agony that such a program would entail if it meant that half the staff would lose their jobs but the business continued to employ the others?

Additionally, more difficult decisions were made as Qantas went through further pain in 2020, with more staff reductions and stand-downs to weather the COVID-19 storm at a time when its major domestic competitor went into voluntary administration. It is very hard to see cost reduction as having a good purpose, but when you see that the difficult and complex choices the business made enabled it to reach its centenary of operations in 2020, then it can evoke pride. What you believe is worthwhile adds meaning to your actions and makes it easier to operate in the complexity.

Meaning helps you rise above the complexity and bring your energy to the project. You are not delivering new trains but rather increasing passenger safety or comfort. You are not building new military helicopters but rather making it more likely that troops will return to their families. Putting customers at the centre of the program makes it easier to realise the significance of what you are doing. When you struggle to find purpose in the project you have underway, you can look to the five basic human ideals that Jim Stengel lays out in his book *Grow* and ask yourself how the project elicits joy, enables connection, inspires exploration, evokes pride or improves society.[19]

Purpose underpins ownership

This might come as a surprise or an annoyance, but the truth is that you can't hold people accountable in complexity. Individuals can only hold themselves accountable (see Box L). When the project is emergent and you can't rely on the plan for direction,

L: The nature of accountability

No one can really hold you accountable. Only you can hold yourself accountable.

During a transformation program, I had a discussion with a consultant about a business lead on one of the workstreams who was not performing. The consultant explained that we needed to write a plan for the leader because he had not delivered in the past six months on the reduction targets. The consultant felt that we had to create a detailed plan, with identified changes, and get the executive to implement it. I explained that this leader had survived many years in the organisation. If we provided the plan he wouldn't argue with it, but in another six months nothing would be done. There might be some apparent signs of progress, but nothing would really change.

The exasperated consultant said we had to hold him accountable. We had to measure his performance, and if he didn't hit the mark after another six months then we would look for his replacement. Given the seniority and specialisation of the role, and the internal process for recruitment, it would take another six months to find someone to fill the role. By this stage we would be one year further down the track with no progress.

The conundrum was that the leader didn't believe in the plan. He didn't believe what we were doing was right. The only way he was ever going to deliver was if he took on board that the transformation was required, important and achievable, at which point he would hold himself accountable – which is what happened when he internalised the value of changing the business, took personal accountability for the results and delivered them ahead of other divisions.

Some would say that teams can hold themselves accountable. It's true that teams can have shared measures and use social pressure to bring forward individual desire to succeed collectively. But the reality is that at any point in time a person can walk away. It all comes down to who you are as a person, what you believe and what standard you hold yourself to.

In complexity, ownership is more effective than accountability in motivating the right actions and behaviours.

ownership of the outcome is the most effective way to coordinate effort and activities.

Ownership means you take on making the result happen even in the absence of clarity or the presence of fear. You are only going to do this if you believe in the purpose of the project. It is a personal choice driven by the meaning you apply to the situation.

You care deeply and are tenacious about delivery when you own the result. It drives you forward through the problems, bringing energy and discretionary effort, and preventing you from being stopped easily. You are emotionally engaged, and have empathy for the users and a relationship with the other team members. It is about not allowing the details to go unnoticed (so everything works on go-live day). It is about having a constant discomfort and desire for things to be better.

However, ownership is not free. When you own the outcomes, you also accept the consequence of not achieving the project – what you miss out on, both individually and collectively. You can't sit on the fence. You can't just be a passive administrator and watch the milestones go whooshing by. Real ownership energises you to deliver the result, even if you don't know how.

Ownership means there is no one else to blame. When you get to design how the project will operate, you decide the rules and you can't complain about the outcome. You are no longer a victim to the situation but have to live with the choices you make and own the consequences of those choices.

Think of the energy difference between when you own an action and when you are directed to take an action. When you are directed, you feel an external obligation; when you own the action, you understand the significance of the action and are compelled to act. As a leader, clarify the purpose and invite ownership, understanding that it means different things to different people. In complexity, certainty of delivery comes from clarity of ownership and consequence, not clarity of plan.

In the absence of standardised procedures and the ability to 'know for sure' in complexity, trust becomes the main organising mechanism. Ownership and trust are two sides of the same coin. If someone is going to own the outcome, you also have to trust them to deliver it. If you don't trust someone, you kill off their energy, creativity and willingness. You diminish ownership when you break trust.

Worth doing well

At the heart of it, with all the emergence and unknowns, being effective in complexity is about what you want to create. Reason is how we find the logic of the situation, but belief is about what we want to create. It is a higher sense of desire. It drives us to be bold. As humans, what we create defines us. It is our legacy; but there is no guarantee we will achieve it.

The project has to be meaningful to make you get up every day in the face of complexity. If the meaning is that you continue to get paid, then maybe that works for you, but it makes it hard to bring others along on the journey. To be effective in complexity, build a belief in the importance of the project so people willingly contribute their energy and passion.

Objectives and plans are useful, but the belief that the project is worthwhile is what makes things happen in complexity. When the project is centred around purpose and ownership, it generates energy and drives progress through the largest obstacles and uncertainties. Belief in the purpose coordinates action and motivates decisions. It is the foundation on which trust is built. It makes it possible to question what is going on without creating chaos and drives you to deliver when you don't know how, or even if, it is possible. It drives staff forward and reduces the frustration of not knowing. It represents the voices outside the project team – the customer, the employee, the stakeholder. It can be wrapped up in a story or a simple measure of success and provide clarity about the consequence of not achieving the outcome. It makes it easier to perform in complexity.

Practices are in tension

Now that you have an understanding of the practices, you might have realised that there is a natural tension on each axis of the model, suggesting actions that appear to be contradictory.

Truth: collective or individual

On the vertical axis, there is a tension between connecting and simplifying (see Figure 7.3). Connecting is the search for greater understanding by increasing the number of opinions and sources. Strong performance comes from increasing the number of views in the room. On the other hand, simplifying is about reducing or distilling what you know down to one thing – a name, a picture or a description that provides insight about the situation. Spending more time connecting will provide a broader view, but eventually arguments become complicated and circular. Moving too quickly to simplifying, on the other hand, will mean your insights are incomplete and decisions could be revisited as more information comes to light.

Figure 7.3: Truth in tension

Time: a resource or a constraint

On the horizontal axis of the model, there is the contradiction between taking time to think and pressing ahead to get things done (see Figure 7.4). The tension between taking the time to hold space and let the answer emerge, and the urgency to keep moving forward and find a way, comes down to a question of time. How much time do you need for exploration and reflection, so that when you move, you are travelling at pace in the right direction? Is time a resource to be used to work out the way forward or a constraint that means you have to move without full information?

Figure 7.4: Time in tension

Resolving the tension

Resolving these tensions is easier when there is clarity of purpose (see Figure 7.5). It also requires judgement and a willingness to get it wrong and try again. There is no algorithm that can be learnt that tells you when the best time is to move between these practices. When do you move forward? When do you hold a bit longer and let the ideas develop? How long should you stay in the conversation, and when do you have enough information to extract the core themes? The purpose of the project will drive you to give decisions the time they need but also push to find a way and get it done.

Figure 7.5: Resolving the tension

This is the art of complex project management – understanding when to move from one practice to another. It is never a serial process with clear boundaries, but rather an arrangement of activities with an emphasis that shifts as you move through the project.

Practices are at the core of the toolkit

The practices of the Complex Project Toolkit stand in contrast to the standard approach to project management (see Table 7.1).

These practices aren't prescriptive activities to be followed like most standard project management approaches. They don't try to create certainty where there isn't any.

Table 7.1: Standard practices versus complexity practices

STANDARD	COMPLEXITY
Scope Be clear, before starting, on what will be delivered	**Connect** The answer evolves and is created by the people involved
Plan Define detailed activities so everyone is clear on their job	**Simplify** An insightful model guides action when surrounded by uncertainty
Track Check progress against plan and take action to bring back on course	**Hold Space** Make time to think and learn because the situation changes
Adjust Tightly manage any changes to minimise variations	**Find a Way** Change the approach to match the situation, anchored in the outcome
Communicate Ensure everyone is aware of their role, accountability and impact	**Purpose** Ownership drives everyone to deliver even they if don't know how

Where the standard toolkit removes ambiguity as soon as possible, creating the problems discussed in Chapter 3, these practices recognise and work with the characteristics of complexity (see Figure 7.6).

These practices are a new, more effective way of operating in complex projects. Standing upon a belief in the purpose of the project, they bring forward ownership, which drives more certainty of delivery in complexity than the standard project management activities and plans. Connecting gives you visibility across the whole landscape. Simplifying ensures that effort is directed towards the most significant issues. Holding space ensures time to think. Finding a way drives you forward even when clarity is lacking. Purpose co-ordinates effort and increases the energy. All of these ensure the project has the best possible chance of success.

Figure 7.6: Complexity characteristics and practices

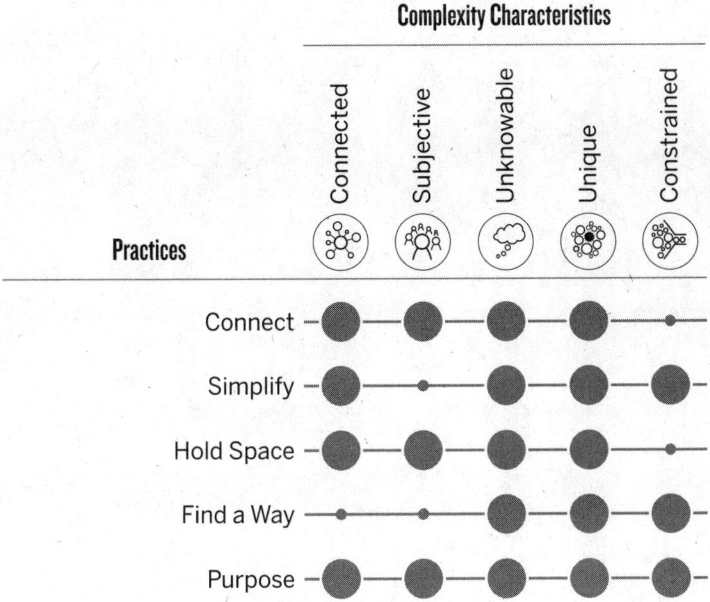

The practices are the core of the Complex Project Toolkit, driving improved performance in complex projects. They rely on the foundation created by the mindsets in Chapter 6 but also require project managers to operate outside their normal comfort zone. This requires new skills, which are covered in the next chapter. Some you might recognise, most come from the designer's toolkit, but they all lift effectiveness in complexity.

Chapter 8
ENHANCED PROJECT SKILLS

'Every skill you acquire doubles your odds of success.'
—Scott Adams

The third element of the Complex Project Toolkit is the skills required to operate effectively. Adopting the mindsets and practices without also taking on the new skills will mean that the toolkit will only occasionally be successful. Without an uplift in capability, there will be moments of brilliance when someone runs a workshop well or redesigns the project approach but, in general, efforts will be ineffective and wasted.

Normal project management skills cover planning and scheduling, communication and controlling costs, risks and quality. These skills support the traditional management functions of planning, organising, staffing, directing and controlling tasks. A search for the skills of complex project managers will reveal that high-level concepts such as creativity, leadership, engagement, innovation and systems thinking are often promoted. One model I came across even included ethics as a core skill. While these aren't wrong per se, they are a bit nebulous. The Complex Project Toolkit has a more focused approach that pinpoints practical skills that emphasise how project managers need to operate in complexity.

The teachable skills of the Complex Project Toolkit fall into three categories (see Figure 8.1). The first is **conversation**, which covers the skills related to bringing people together to build a collective view of the situation or generate agreement on the way forward. The second is **sense-making**, which supports how we understand, reorganise and simplify what we encounter in the program. Both of these come directly from the designer's toolkit and are not normally associated with project management. The final group is the **adaption** skills, which create the ability to deliver the project even though everything seems to be unstable. This includes both design-driven skills and some that will be familiar to experienced project managers.

Figure 8.1: Skills of the Complex Project Toolkit

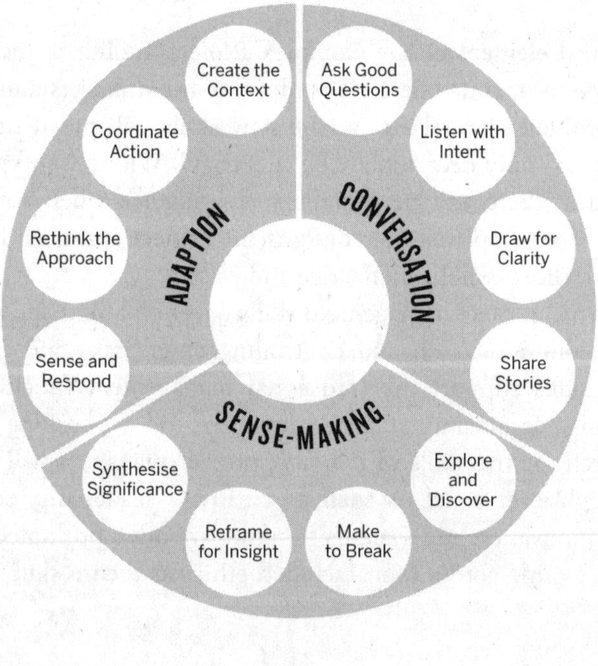

When defining this set of skills, the hope was to align them to the practices. As it turned out, some relate to specific practices but most support a variety of them and rely on a range of mindsets. For example, 'listen with intent', which is part of the 'conversation' category, is how we build a collective view about the situation ('connect') or generate agreement on an approach ('find a way') and relies on the mindset of 'give up knowing'. As a result, there is no simple mapping between the three elements of the toolkit, even though at times it might feel like there could be.

The skills of the Complex Project Toolkit are in addition to the normal project skill-set and expand a project manager's ability to operate well in high levels of complexity.

The intent here is not to make designers out of project managers, but rather to give them a grounding in the design skills that will help them address the characteristics of complexity and increase their likelihood of success.

Conversation

Conversation is at the heart of the humanity of this toolkit, and of the ability to succeed in complexity. I'm not talking about a bit of a chat, but rather a deep interaction that brings to the fore potentially hidden issues and differences of opinion. Conversation is how we come to understand one another's realities and collectively define the situation. David Whyte mentions in his book *Crossing the Unknown Sea* that 'I can measure the brain but it is only in conversation that I understand the mind'.[1]

Conversation is the best way to connect with others and generate collective wisdom, understand the systemic implications of decisions or actions and deal with the messy connectedness of complexity. Conversation creates content, shares meaning and surfaces issues.

A real conversation allows the discussion to be guided by whatever emerges. It is not about sticking to a predefined process or schedule, but about being immersed in the topic, listening for what is important to those in the room and seeing where it leads you. You might create an agenda to provide guidance for the discussion, but don't be confined by it. You can probably imagine how frustrating this can be for some people, but you need to be open to what materialises and follow the energy of the conversation.

When running a conversation, you have to make sure you have got the right people involved, because the perspectives of those in the room define reality. Ask yourself: is every aspect of this multidisciplinary situation represented, including individuals with experience, the naysayers, those with the bright ideas and those who are passionate about the topic?

At the heart of facilitating a good conversation is the ability to ask good questions, listen well and use the power of visual aids and stories to capture the nuances of the project.

Ask good questions

Given that perspectives define what is real, and truth is created through discussion and debate, only by asking good questions do we understand what is true for a particular group at a specific time. Questions and their answers are how we create new knowledge.

How many times have you been in a meeting that goes round and round, or completely misses the point, because no one is asking the right question? Have you felt the cut-through when someone asks the insightful question that gets right to the heart of the matter? It is easy to waste time and energy and thought and analysis on a topic because no one takes the time to ask the right questions.

But how do you know if you are asking a good question? There are a number of frameworks that go beyond simplistic closed questions that draw a yes/no answer ('Did you have a good day?') and open questions that elicit a more detailed response ('What sort of day did you have?').

A good place to start is with the six types of Socratic questions:

1. Questions for clarification
2. Questions that probe assumptions
3. Questions that probe for reasons and evidence
4. Questions about viewpoints and perspectives
5. Questions that probe implications and consequences
6. Questions about the question.

Incidentally, Socrates talked about the need to protect the independent thinker. This is something to consider in complexity. If someone thinks differently, take the time to listen to them and understand their position rather than dismissing them as a lone nut.

An example of using good questions is the after action review (AAR) developed by the US military for assessing performance in training exercises. It is based on four insightful questions: What was expected to happen? What actually occurred? What went well, and why? What can be improved, and how? Simple and clear. Once these questions have been answered, we have created a collective truth about the situation; we all have the same understanding.

While the AAR focuses on questions about the past, there are different ways to think about the future. Author Mark Strom distinguishes between an abstract and a grounded question.[2] An abstract question is external to the individual ('What do we need to fix in this school?') and focuses on getting to answers. But the answers it elicits will often diverge based on opinions. A grounded question draws out meaning and stories ('Why did you become a teacher?') and provides a much stronger base from which to converge on a course of action. Grounded questions are at the heart of finding purpose and meaning in the situation because they focus on something an individual relates to that draws them forward into a different future.

Whatever structure you use, good questions come from giving up knowing and embracing real curiosity. Your task as the project manager is to generate understanding in the group, not just to apply your existing meaning.

Listen with intent

There is no point coming up with a good question if you don't listen to the answer. If you ask questions, at least have the courtesy to listen to the responses. Listening is a gift that shows you respect the speaker enough to open up to their reality.

Most people are unaware that you can manage your listening. This isn't just about being attentive and not daydreaming while someone is talking. Managing your listening is an active process of being aware of both what the person is saying and also how you are reacting to it.

One of the most famous frameworks for managing how you listen to a conversation is Edward de Bono's Six Thinking Hats. In this model, different coloured hats represent different ways of thinking about a situation and can used to direct what you are listening for – red is emotions and ego, white is information, and so on. This is used to organise groups in how they are processing what someone is saying. For example, 'black hat' sessions are used to look for fault in the topic of discussion. Attendees, including whoever created the content, are clear on the intent and manage their listening accordingly.[3]

I came across another framework for managing listening while working at CSC Index that distinguishes between 'automatic' and 'generative' listening.

Automatic listening is what we normally fall into. It could be because we are rushed or uninterested, and you will probably recognise some of its traits. It is when your focus is on identifying your view on the topic and speaker. 'What is the fatal flaw in their argument?' 'Yeah, but…' 'How can I use what they are saying?' 'Are they done yet?' 'Is there a gap so I can make my point?'

All of these represent your mind being in your world and not in the conversation.

Generative listening, on the other hand, is focused on the speaker. You are listening for the other person's brilliance, or their commitment, or their wisdom of experience, or deeply trying to understand the point they are making. This mode of listening is more engaging, and the speaker will feel heard and honoured.

Generative listening helps you understand where someone comes from. When you take the time to understand someone's argument, not only do you learn their point of view but it also becomes easier to converge upon a topic. When you understand where someone is coming from, you can provide a different lens to their own view of the situation, which is more effective than opposing their view directly.

Skills as a listener can range from very simple (letting the person finish) to advanced (managing your listening). The conversation can be improved by swapping out 'yeah, but...' with 'yes, and...' – an old technique from improv theatre to keep things moving forward. The ability to listen well to others is a fundamental skill in conversation.

Draw for clarity

This is a scenario that plays out time and time again in projects. A project is underway and there are disagreements about when the result will be delivered. Different parties have different views on how long things will take, or about issues that are in the way or yet to be addressed. Mapping out the timeline and all the identified issues, normally on a large whiteboard, brings all the opinions together and generates alignment on the ability to achieve the deadline on the current path. If things are getting off track, the visual aid highlights where improvement is required in order to achieve the target. This map on the wall changes the conversation from an argument about what each person believes to be the likely delivery date to a discussion in which the team designs what needs to be done to make it happen.

A timeline is a classic project visual. But the use of visuals extends far beyond this simple concept. Done well, visuals make it easier to think collectively. They crystallise ideas and make them visible in conversations. Whether it is understanding connections across the project, explaining complex technical topics or sorting out what is the most significant constraint, drawings communicate ideas and concepts – particularly complex and connected ones – faster and more accurately than words alone. Drawings are a critical element of facilitating good conversations because they bring together the disparate points of view and can ensure everyone is on the same page. Misconceptions can be identified and dealt with much faster by drawing than by just talking about the situation. Explaining ideas with words alone can spiral into semantics on the meaning of particular phrases or the interpretation of words. A drawing externalises the idea from the individual who raised it so the concept becomes the focus of attention, driving a more meaningful debate.

Drawing your idea can also make you smarter. In 1987, Jill Larkin and Herbert Simon put forward the concept of 'finite fuel', where the power of your brain is split between understanding a problem and processing it.[4] The faster you can understand, the more capacity you have for processing (see Figure 8.2). Drawings reduce the load on the 'understanding' part to create more capacity for processing, because they can represent complex concepts in a simple form. I proved this point many times in part of a university activity I ran, where I gave teams the example problem in Larkin and Simon's paper. Some received the problem in text only, while others were also given a diagram. Those with the diagram always finished faster and with greater accuracy. Often the first step for those who were given just the text was to draw a diagram.

Figure 8.2: Finite fuel

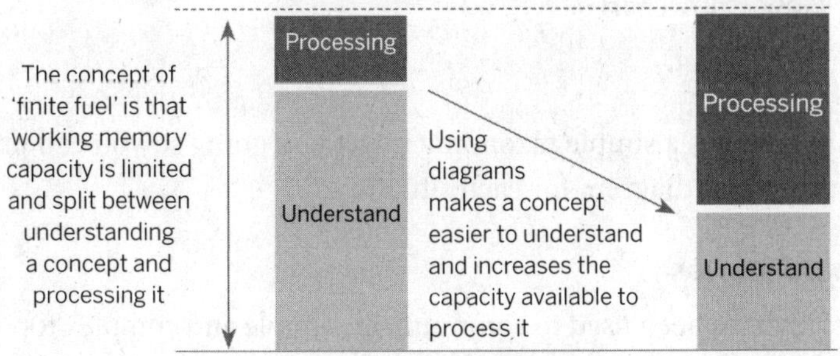

Cognitive scientists refer to concepts we can easily understand as having 'processing fluency'. Bob Nease wrote, 'The greater something's "fluency," the more we tend to like it, the less risky we judge it, the more popular and prevalent we believe it is, and the easier we think it is to do.'[5] Diagrams can increase the fluency of an idea.

You don't need to be an artist or cartoonist to be good at visuals. You don't need to create stunning graphical representations. It is about finding a visual means of cutting through the complexity of the situation. The main thing is to try and retry. Rarely does the first drawing survive until the end of the conversation. Draw something, work out what is missing, draw something else – keep moving until you find the insight that resonates for you. Drawing is a simple tool that helps people think together.

Developing your visual vocabulary with some simple techniques will help you get better at drawing in conversations. Dan Roam's book *The Back of the Napkin* is a great source to get you moving on visualisation of ideas.[6] He talks about six things you see and the corresponding six diagrams that relate to them:

1. Who/what – portrait
2. How much – chart
3. Where – map

4. When – timeline
5. How – flowchart
6. Why – plot.

This provides a simple taxonomy to get you going so you can pull out the right diagram for each situation.

Share stories

Stories have been used to communicate simple and complex topics for millennia. They are the most basic way we have of interacting with one another and are one of the best ways to understand or communicate a complex topic. Storytelling stimulates different parts of the brain than analytics – those involved in attention, learning and empathy, which are most useful when trying to understand or explain complex topics.[7] Stories help us form a deep, nuanced picture of the situation.

Adam, a frontline worker in an engineering company, told me his story about being retrenched. He was on holiday, riding his motorbike through a wilderness area on the trip of a lifetime. He stopped at a small pub for the night. He had a couple of drinks at the bar and went upstairs to get ready for dinner. It was then that he saw an email telling him he was retrenched. He had no idea this was coming. His job meant so much to him. He was a good worker – how could this happen? When he came back down, the publican saw something was wrong. Adam told him what had happened. The publican sorted his last few customers, shut the doors and spent the evening drinking and chatting with Adam.

Adam told me that the publican saved him that night. He was thousands of miles from home and didn't feel he had anything to go back to, having just lost the job he loved. He didn't know what he would have done had he not had that chance to vent. The publican's empathy that night gave him a whole new perspective of the world that put Adam in the right frame of mind to make it home safely.

Take a moment to reflect on this story. What do you take from it? You might see the value of empathy and looking out for the mental health of others, or the resilience of people to get back up after adversity. For me, this story is about the potential impact of the way we communicate significant changes to people. If I was running a program that involved redundancies, I could demand that you issue all notices face-to-face and hope you comply. Alternatively, I could tell you this story about the significance of the way we communicate change and, as a result, feel confident that you will do whatever it takes to ensure a callous approach never occurs on your watch.

Stories provide insight into the speaker. The flow, focus and point of view of the narrative provide clues to their world view and what is meaningful for them. Stories communicate our values and are how we can uncover the humanity of the situation. As discussed in the last chapter, stories are full of information beyond just the basic facts. We can't help but interpret a story in our own way and extract our own meaning from it.

Stories make it easier to recall details. Research has shown that 'character-driven stories with emotional content result in a better understanding of the key points a speaker wishes to make and enable better recall of these points weeks later'.[8] If you heard Adam tell his story, you would not easily forget it.

Sharing stories is not about being humorous or a raconteur. It is about using a simple technique to cut through the complexity to illuminate the nuances of a situation. There are a range of archetypes and guidelines for storytelling (like Freytag's Pyramid and story arcs), but don't overthink it. Just about everyone can tell a story. Try it if you are struggling to get your point across. The easiest stories to tell are those from your personal experience. Getting better at storytelling has more to do with clarity and empathy than anything else. Be clear on the point you want to make, and understand the mindset of your audience and what they are interested in.

The challenge for the complex project manager is being able to draw stories out from others, to derive meaning from what you hear and find the stories that best embody the significant message. As with drawings, it often takes a while to find the good stories, so don't stop looking.

Asking good questions, listening with intent, drawing for clarity and sharing stories are the four skills at the heart of the 'conversation' category. The skills need to be developed, however many things get in the way, especially impatience and the feeling that we 'don't have time for this'. Many people operating in projects don't value stories as highly as data and only use visuals to make sure everyone else understands their ideas. Conversation generates the connections required to address the characteristics of complexity and operate effectively.

Sense-making

'Sense-making' is a term commonly used by designers. It is a structured analysis of the environment to gain a deeper understanding and identify what is important. Complex projects require skills in sense-making because of the inability to define everything upfront. Much of the time spent in complex projects is about understanding what you have, 'making sense' of the environment and using that understanding to focus action in the right direction.

Making sense of a connected and evolving situation is a skill that managers of complex projects need to master. The boundaries of the project can be fuzzy and the levers for improvement unknown, and information continues to emerge.

Sense-making involves the ability to discover divergent information, find new ways of looking at the problem, identify what is significant and then bring it all together in a synthesised description to make it easier to understand the whole situation.

Explore and discover

The ability to explore and discover underpins the search for insights and breakthroughs that come from expanding your view beyond the immediate environment. It starts with looking past the boundaries of the current system in focus to understand the broader context. This opens your mind to other possibilities and makes it easier to see and question the underlying belief system, as Alexis did in the example of the project status room in Chapter 4. This is the antithesis of documenting scope to focus the project on solving a particular problem.

Exploration and discovery are at the heart of the Double Diamond model introduced in Chapter 5. The divergence at the start of each diamond depends on your ability to open up options rather than trying to constrain them.

At the core of exploring and discovering are the willingness to look outside what would normally be considered relevant areas of focus, and the capability to interpret what you find there. You also need to bring what you find back to something meaningful and relevant to the project. Exploration can provide insight into what is missing from the current world views, or more effective ways of operating that can deliver the result faster.

In her book *How to Be an Explorer of the World*, Keri Smith provides a great list for discovering what is going on around you.[9] A few points worth calling out are:

- Always be looking.
- Everything is interesting. Look closer.
- Notice the stories going on around you.
- Notice patterns, make connections.
- Trace things back to their origins.

Much of this skill is about being present to what is happening in your orbit and being able to notice things beyond the obvious. You can see the correlation with the 'Always curious' mindset.

Performing this skill well requires you to rise above cognitive blind spots like bounded rationality (where you limit the range of options considered) and selective attention, which can lead you to miss significant information. The classic demonstration of selective attention is the 'invisible gorilla' experiment, in which research psychologists Daniel Simons and Christopher Chabris had students watch a video of basketball players and count the number of passes between players of one team. Remarkably, only 50% reported noticing a man in a full gorilla suit walk slowly across the court in the middle of the game.[10] The researchers' purpose was to test the phenomenon of inattentional blindness. The point is that it is very easy to be so focused on the immediate that you miss something of significance.

To exercise these skills in full, you need to draw upon the practice of holding space by suspending judgement while the search continues. This can be exasperating for those who believe they know the answer. It can appear to be an aimless wander through apparently unrelated ideas rather than a directed path towards a defined goal. You need the ability to follow up interesting leads but also the drive to move towards an outcome.

Make to break (and learn)

Designers use the expression 'make to learn and learn to make' to refer to the activity of constructing something specific to represent ideas and learning from that to revise the ideas. This is part of the move between abstract (concept) and specific (construction) that is one of the traits of design thinking. Activities covered by this expression include building prototypes and running pilots. 'Making' crystallises the ideas into something that can be debated and progressed. Done well, it externalises the debate away from individuals and anchors discussion on the ideas.

In the standard approach to projects, the purpose of a prototype is to prove the system or process works – to prove you have it right in order to reduce risk during implementation. You are done when the process or product being tested meets all the defined criteria.

In complexity, the focus is on learning, not proving what you know. It is about finding out what is wrong with your current solution, finding out where it breaks. You want to understand the limits of the system to prove its validity. There is more information in breaking something than operating it properly. This is a subtle but significant difference. Rather than run a pilot to show off what has been created, run a 'lab' to test the ideas and see what can be found wanting. It is about experimentation rather than confirmation, and the ability to do this is important in complexity because so many unknowns need to be shaken out.

An airline was testing out a new passenger boarding process. Testing of the new process was carried out in a live operational environment before rolling it out. The focus was not on checking if the design worked, but rather on looking for potential problems. The question was not 'Will it work?' but 'How could it fail?' Without this approach to the complexity of dealing with the travelling public, many issues could have arisen during the implementation that would have required it to be put on hold or even cancelled.

'Making' skills are about the ability to construct an object, whether that is a physical model, a diagram of the overall process or even a point of view (mentioned in Box L back on page 161) – anything that makes the abstract more concrete. Breaking is as much about an attitude towards what has been created as it is about the specific set of skills required. This attitude is the willingness to break something down, to accept it only as a transitional item and then destroy what has been created for the purpose of learning. Doing this could mess with a project plan because the activity might take longer, or it might be faster than planned. The point of the exercise, though, is learning early to save time later.

Making something and then trying to find out why it doesn't work provides insight into the whole system. It helps to identify what people are passionate about, where the limits are and what the key connections might be.

Reframe for insight

We all have a frame through which we view the world. Something that sets humans apart from other animals is our ability to build a model of the world in our minds. This model is a product of our upbringing, education and experiences. We understand complex concepts by framing them within the model we have built up over time. The simplifying power of this model is also its downside in that it can restrict our ability to go beyond what we know. As mentioned in Chapter 2, the HR manager defines the problem as driven by culture and capability; the IT person sees holes in the data architecture and security. Reframing recognises that our framing limits possibility and that changing the model can bring a powerful new perspective that opens up insights and possibilities.

Reframing well requires the ability to recognise the limits of your own view of the situation and open yourself up to alternative perspectives that can provide more insight. At its heart, reframing brings different lenses to bear on a situation, which improves understanding and expands thinking about the topic. Academics Sara Beckmann and Michael Barry describe reframing the problem definition as a critical part of the search for emergent opportunities.[11]

The best way to step outside your existing mental model, whether to understand the world better or to develop a collective truth, is through the use of metaphors. The power of the metaphor is to bring concepts from one world into another. Metaphors can help explain a situation or generate insight. In *A Whole New*

Mind, Daniel H. Pink talks about how, 'In a complex world, mastery of metaphor… has become more valuable.'[12]

If I say a complex project is like putting together a massive LEGO set without instructions, it immediately forms a 'picture' in your mind. It doesn't matter if it's right; it has formed an image you can run with. That is the power of metaphor – to bring on a debate about something complex by using a picture of something already known.

Metaphors open up new views and new ways of framing the situation within the group. Think about the metaphor 'war on drugs'. The moment 'war' is mentioned, you visualise the mobilisation of military force, a high level of spending, a significant issue for the country and a long timeframe. If the naming was 'the medical emergency of drugs', then it would conjure up a more remedial, compassionate and science-based approach.

The right metaphor can generate a much broader understanding of a complex situation. For example, a simple metaphor that works well when implementing a new IT system is to compare it to renovating a house. Is the plan to go from room to room, touching up the paint, adding new curtains and furniture (new desktop computers and an upgraded operating system), or is the plan to rebuild from the foundations, rewiring the whole house (new large system implementation)? From this simple starting point, everyone can begin extending the metaphor. For example, implementing a whole new system could be described as building a new place next door, and sometime in the future we will move in, but only a few rooms at a time (migrate accounting first, followed by payroll and then operations after that). At some point we will be operating between the two houses (we'll need to work on both systems), so some compromise will be required. You can imagine how this metaphor can be extended in different ways to help everyone understand the nature of the transition and the pieces that need to come together. In this way the metaphor can communicate a complex idea succinctly.

While helping us understand a situation in a more nuanced way, metaphors can also open up creativity around the topic, which in turn leads to new insights. If you are trying to get your team to think more broadly to reframe the situation, you need to activate the creative centre of the brain to develop ideas. A simple technique is to start the discussion by asking everyone to come up with as many uses as possible for a common item, like a brick or a blanket. It should come as no surprise that young children, unencumbered by societal norms, are best at this.

The key skill for project managers when it comes to metaphors is both to encourage team members to generate them and to build their ability to recognise a good one that provides leverage and insight. If the particular metaphor isn't working, change it. You have probably experienced a situation in which a metaphor was taken too far. Don't get attached to them. If a metaphor ceases to be useful, keep moving until you find one that works. Look for metaphors that work for the specific problem you are dealing with but also for the whole environment.

Synthesise significance

Synthesis is about distilling all you have found down to a few insightful points, or a killer picture, or a simple explanation that is concise and compelling and perfectly encapsulates the situation. It is more than just recognising previous patterns and grouping what you know into categories and recommendations.

Where reframing breaks away from our current understanding, synthesis brings forward a new view that galvanises and drives action. It organises, shapes and trims what you know in order to highlight the most important points. It is a search for significance that finishes when it exposes gaps in your understanding and provides insight into the whole situation. Synthesis is not just sorting into categories but looking for themes that run through the topics and crystallise a compelling argument. A strong synthesis creates an 'aha' moment when something previously hidden comes into view and makes the path forward clear, concise and compelling. It takes perseverance and patience and multiple iterations, rather than locking in the first idea that comes along in order to remove the uncertainty as quickly as possible.

The importance of synthesis can't be overstated in complexity. It is a core skill of the 'simplify' practice. When done well, it brings together all the disparate views and cuts through the fog to provide a level of clarity that makes it easier to operate. Without synthesis, we can be left chasing down unimportant details and frustrated by effort that doesn't make a difference. Big brains look for more detail; smart brains look for significance.

While synthesis can sometimes appear to be magical, there are techniques that can be taught: information layering, zooming in and out, identifying themes and making judgements are all synthetic skills known to strategists and designers.

The concept of **information layering** comes from *The Pyramid Principle* by Barbara Minto (see Box M, overleaf), which outlines a technique for structuring thinking and presenting ideas clearly.[13] Creating a pyramid of information – with the answer or core concept at the top and more and more detail being added as you move down through the layers – makes it easier to recognise the level and significance of what you have in view. Technicians struggle with the search for significance because they see every part of the system as equally important – nothing can be left out, and there isn't a clear process to follow. By layering the problem you can focus on the few things that matter – the core topics, the key constraint, the high-leverage actions – rather than spreading your efforts across everything.

Zoom in, zoom out, a phrase coined by Rosabeth Moss Kanter in a 2011 *Harvard Business Review* article of the same name, refers to the technique of moving between viewing the bigger picture and closing in on details, depending on what is required.[14] The ability to move between these different levels of seeing and understanding helps to identify what is important and what is superfluous.

M: Information layering

Information layering is based on the finding that most people can hold only five to seven ideas in their working memory at any one time, and if there are more items then they need to be grouped to be comprehended.

Imagine stepping into a project that is in trouble. There are dozens of issues, but where do you put the focus? What do you address first? If you address individual issues one at a time, you will be swamped and likely miss an issue of significance.

You might find that all the issues can be grouped into categories – governance, staffing and communication, for example. This is the first layer. Within this, you might find the vast majority of issues relate to staffing. You group them thematically, forming a second layer (see Figure 8.3). Again, within this group you can identify the most significant issue and focus on addressing it.

The point here is not just about the focus: the other areas don't get ignored. What you have done is identified a high leverage point for addressing issues and formed a structure to identify significance when new issues arise.

Creating the layering requires you to promote some concepts and demote others. The real art is finding the themes without overlap. The connected nature of complexity can make this hard, however the aim is to structure your thinking to see the whole picture but also dive into the detail where required. Then you can focus on areas of significance without missing anything.

Figure 8.3: Information layering

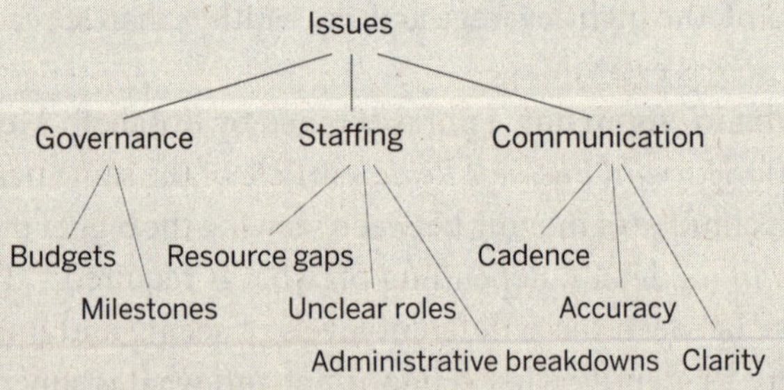

Synthesis is also about **identifying significant themes** that pervade the project. This starts with grouping ideas into categories, best done by physically moving things around either on a whiteboard or with Post-it notes. But it doesn't stop there. At this point all you have done is replay what you have seen or been told. Insight and impact comes from looking across the categories to find underlying themes that are initially hidden but explain gaps or assumptions that aren't working.

For example, say that the analysis of a program grouped issues into budget, timing and risk categories. It showed that on average, projects were forecasting 5% under budget, risk profiles were reasonable, but timelines were slipping and projects were having lots of apparently unconnected issues. Each of the issues was identified and grouped to look for common causes. Standing back and synthesising the situation, the problem was that most projects were run by operational managers without project experience. They knew how to look after a budget and fix problems as they arose, but they lacked the skills to stay ahead of the problems. The most effective solution to many of the problems was to lift the understanding and skill level of the project leaders.

Synthesis starts with wondering, trying out different ideas and diagrams highlighting alternative structures and relationships. Ideally, at some point, there is a moment when you realise you have been looking at the whole situation the wrong way. This is the moment when you see that all the things you have been doing are not addressing the real problem. In *Strategic Intuition*, William Duggan talks about having the presence to recognise the flash of insight when it occurs.[15]

The final technique in synthesis is **judgement**, where you make a call without full information. How do you know you have layered the problem well? How do you know you have seen all the connections? You don't. Experience helps (because good decisions are often built upon the ashes of bad decisions), but this is where abductive thinking comes in – what do you believe is the best explanation or description? It helps to look for 'resonance', where the same theme or framing keeps recurring as you spend time with a topic, not because you are fixated on it but because it is raised by different people independently and continues to make sense the more you look at it.

Events such as reviews or demonstrations can also accelerate the synthesis process and drive it to conclusion. There is a famous saying that design is never done, it just becomes due. Creating events to present what has been made or debate the result, regardless of the state it is in, forces the ideas to take form.

For those of you looking for a simple 'how to' guide, this is where it breaks down. There is no certainty in the call you make in complexity. You need to move when it feels right and be willing to adjust as you learn.

Synthesis, more than most of the skills in the Complex Project Toolkit, requires practice and the right frame of mind. Complex project managers need to be willing to sit with the problems and make the call to move forward when it feels right.

Sense-making comes straight out of the designer's toolkit. These skills are significantly different from the normal project skills, which can create resistance to these ideas in a project environment. But the reality is that the chance of a successful project outcome increases when a team has the skills to cut through the complexity and focus on the things that matter.

Adaption

The final set of skills provides the ability to deliver results in a changing environment. Standard project management skills are rooted in the delivery of a known object. They focus on delivering against the plan and actively managing any potential risks of variation. They are about providing visibility of what is going on and controlling variation when things get off track.

The adaption skills in the Complex Project Toolkit supplement the normal project management list and underpin how you deliver successfully when the world keeps changing. They are based on the idea that the project has to morph constantly to fit the situation as understanding improves, but also that the situation can be moulded to improve the chance of success.

Sense and respond

The Normandy landings in June 1944 were the largest seaborne invasion in history. They also involved 24,000 airborne troops. One of the issues with this many paratroopers was how to maintain coherence of the field units. Wind, incorrectly placed beacons, obstacles and injuries would scatter troops across the landing zone, some taking days to be reunited with their units. Given the large numbers, a simple order was issued. On landing, form up in fighting units with those around you. Sense what you have and respond to the situation in front of you, working towards the overall objective.

Sensing and responding is about adjusting the project to what you see occurring. It is the opposite of ensuring adherence to a plan. The ability to sense what is happening and respond as the situation emerges is essential in complexity, given that many things are unknowable, particularly early in the project. It might mean modifying the approach (see the next skill, 'Rethink the approach'), or changing the team, or moving to a new location – whatever it takes to make sure the project is optimised for the setting as it is revealed.

This skill is the ability to read the situation, to recognise whether something is significant and requires action or can be ignored, and then to respond at the right level.

Projects will always have issues and many of them will grow exponentially if they are ignored. I often talk to project managers about the importance of being willing to have lots of small explosions (where issues are openly discussed and addressed) followed by course corrections, rather than ignoring or minimising problems until they can't be hidden anymore and create one big explosion that demands attention. If the first workshop in a series designing new processes doesn't go well, it is better to address the problem immediately and adjust the approach rather than assuming it will get better over the course of the project. Many of the Airbus A380 development issues described in Chapter 6 were flagged well ahead of time, but for whatever reason there was either an inability or an unwillingness to address the problems until they became significant and blew out the schedule, adding millions to the project cost.

The ability to sense what is happening depends on the connections and relationships you have established throughout the project and the wider environment. Are you connected to the various teams and stakeholders? Are you listening to what is emerging in and around the project? Have you established the trust that encourages everyone to bring issues forward?

In order to recognise what is significant, you need to build an appreciation of the technical details of the project, the outcomes and constraints. A lot has been written about the negative impact of moving Boeing's headquarters from Seattle to Chicago and in creating that geographical distance between management and manufacturing.[16] In the move, senior executives lost the connection with the frontline: the ability to wander the floor in the manufacturing facility and sense what was really going on.

Here's another tip. If you are using the contract as the key way to manage the customer–supplier relationship in the project, you are not sensing what is really going on. You are stuck in the past and the project will be in deep trouble, either now or in the near future.

Rethink the approach

Given that complex projects emerge over time, we need the willingness and ability to step back and change tactics as we learn more about the situation. This is not about blindly trying a different path when things don't go well; rather, it is about making a deliberate assessment of the model that underpins the current way of proceeding. The aim in rethinking the approach is to create a plan that delivers the project in the best way possible but is also grounded in the current reality.

The first part of this skill is a willingness to be agnostic about the current approach. Most project managers develop a work breakdown structure that lays out all of the activities to be performed. Whether they realise it or not, this locks in how they think about the problem. The more detailed the breakdown structure, the more comfort they have that they know everything that needs to be done, and the more attached they are to it because of the effort required to create it. This makes it very difficult to suggest alternative framings.

When a multi-billion-dollar program for the refit of a fleet of warships was initiated, the plan called for the completion of one ship per year. The program manager had a 30,000-line project plan that detailed all the activities to be performed. When reality hit and the program started to fall behind, the focus of the team was to execute the identified tasks faster to bring it back on track. This, predictably, made things worse, and the project fell further and further behind. The project needed to rethink the overall approach.

With a focus on getting the ships back to sea with as much capability as possible, the original approach of allocating detailed tasks to trade-based teams was dropped in favour of delivering six workstreams producing large functional components. This layered the problem, reduced complexity and made it obvious that only two of the workstreams were really causing the delay. Those two workstreams were redesigned to remove dependencies and speed up return to service. For example, the information technology stream was broken up into a number of releases to relaunch the ship as soon as possible, with further updates delivered later. Some rework was involved, as the ship would need to return every few months for updates, but this was a small price to pay when compared with having it sitting in dry dock for months on end.

A core technique for rethinking the approach is 'right-to-left planning'. This starts with the outcome in mind, identifies the key constraints and core features of the environment and then works back to identify 'what needs to be true' to meet this result. While having this freedom of thought, it is also important to ground the answer within the reality of the situation, as part of this skill is the ability to identify which constraints are real and which can be questioned.

At some point when redesigning an approach, you will find there are issues or constraints you have to accept. What Bill Burnett calls 'gravity problems' are those that can be a frustration but are not really a problem because there are no actions that can affect them.[17] Contract probity requirements are an example – they might feel like they are getting in the way of moving forward at pace, but they need to be accepted as the way of doing business. The skill here is to recognise which constraints are real and not expend energy on trying to combat them.

On another project I worked on, we knew that the plan we started with would only be valid for a few weeks as priorities shifted and information emerged. We took what we called a 'low fidelity' approach – enough information to drive action but not so much that we wasted time on detail that would change. We also kept it flexible enough that most of the team would be focused on the main game while smaller groups would be dispatched to deal with hotspot issues or conflicts.

Rethinking the approach can be done at all levels of a project. As discussed in previous chapters, the conversational rather than document-based approach in signing off the train design created a better result faster, as did the $200,000 process change rather than the $2 million software implementation to solve an insurance company reconciliation issue. The results were achieved faster, at lower cost and higher quality than the original approach.

Coordinate action

In normal projects, the plan plays a crucial role in coordinating action across large groups of people. But when the plan changes often and so many things are open to interpretation, new skills need to be developed and new methods need to be used to ensure everyone is moving in the same direction.

Coordinating action in complexity moves everything from the document-based paradigm of the standard project approach to more personal and interactive methods. The skills required to operate well in this environment revolve around building relationships with informal communication networks, establishing trust so that teams don't need full information before they move, and working on alignment so everyone is moving in the same direction even in uncertainty.

As the project manager, you need to encourage everyone to take action around more face-to-face conversations and building their informal network. In complex projects, relationships within the team and with stakeholders carry much of the load, rather than prescribed processes. Addressing issues can't be based on putting together a briefing document, sending it to someone for comment and then waiting a week for feedback. You need to get out and talk to people to get a nuanced understanding of the situation. When someone in a project complains that they don't know what is happening on a particular workstream, they need to go and talk to the team about it and not just wait for the formal process of the next meeting. In the emergent world of complexity, the way of coordinating action moves from formal to informal, from monthly steering committees to weekly catch-ups, daily check-ins and even ad-hoc calls.

These relationships also form the basis of trust, which is fundamental in coordinating action in uncertainty. Trust is how you get the team to move even when you can't provide clarity. In an emerging situation I saw a manager tell a team member, 'I need you to fly to the Adelaide office and be on standby, but I can't tell you any more at this stage.' With no further information, he was willing to go, because of the trust that had been built up and because he had ownership of the outcome.

Given the emergent condition of complex projects, with the potential to misread the situation, alignment of understanding amongst the players is critical. Alignment means everyone has the same broad understanding of the project and purpose, and clarity of their role as it exists today. As the program leader, it is your job to check in with everyone to ensure they have the right interpretation of what is occurring. This comes not from documentation but from having everyone exposed to the same information and involved in the discussions about findings and implications. Meetings are more about sharing information and stories than checking in on progress. Diagrams are useful in clarifying understanding and driving out any misalignment that comes from 'lazy' language that is open to misinterpretation.

All of this requires a solid foundation for the relationships within the team. With trust built between the team members, there is more space for risk-taking, making challenging requests and providing direct feedback.

Create the context

The 'context' is the environment the project is operating in. It is the political situation, the amount of free rein given by the owners, and the nature and influence of the stakeholders on the project. Most project managers understand that they have to manage the context of the project and ensure key stakeholders are kept up to date on a regular basis.

But many project managers miss the fact that in complexity, you don't have to accept the context as it is. The situation is evolving, and you have the ability to actively manage opinions and perspectives and thereby create the context that works best for you. The way you operate, your ability to warn of impending issues and how far out in front of the problem you operate all change the environment you are operating in.

Creating context is a higher-order skill. It involves actively educating and influencing stakeholders so they are prepared for and support any changes in the approach. Done well, the stakeholders will understand the situation and actively participate to ensure the conditions for success are in place. It is important to make sure that stakeholders don't have the wrong perception of what is going on, so that you are able to hold space and not spend your time fighting fires and dealing with concerns about the lack of certainty.

I've often described this skill as a process of earning and using credits. By delivering on your word in complex situations, by showing integrity, you build trust. At some point you use that backing to make a call that others might not agree with, but they trust you to do the right thing. This is how you can create 'air cover' to do the things you see need to be done but which might not fit the normal playbook. It allows you to bend the context to how you need it to be. It can also create a level of patience from executives, giving you time to hold off on providing an answer or outcome until the work has been done.

Project managers often complain about the number of meetings they must attend and how little they achieve. As the program manager in complexity, most meetings are not for you, and they are not intended to help you deliver the 'stuff'. The meetings create the context that allows you to get stuff done without distraction.

The adaption skills of the Complex Project Toolkit are anchored in the project management reality of getting things done. They reflect the importance of being in action, of being assertive, when the environment is emerging. The skills require you to 'trust your gut', use judgement and be fixated on the outcome. Experienced project managers will recognise some of these skills and are likely to practise them already. When combined with the other skill-sets in the toolkit, they are a powerful force in improving complex project delivery.

Rounding out the toolkit

The archetype of standard project management skills is aimed at the logistics of the project – communicating, planning, scheduling, measuring, controlling, and so on. They stand on the fact that we have decided what we are building and can now focus on the execution.

The skills of the Complex Project Toolkit are based on the realisation that the way forward is not yet known, and that learning doesn't stop during delivery. These skills (as shown in Table 8.1) supplement standard project management competencies and enhance your ability to deal with complex and emergent situations. They are informed by design thinking, align with the characteristics of complexity (as shown in Figure 8.4) and make it easier to succeed in the creative, rather than mechanistic, environments of complex projects.

These skills round out the Complex Project Toolkit. Used in conjunction with the mindsets and practices, they create a new operating model that increases the probability of success in complex projects. Implementing the entire toolkit takes time and, more significantly, requires giving up habits learned over many years. Making this transition is the focus of the next chapter.

Table 8.1: Standard versus complexity skills

STANDARD	COMPLEXITY
Communication Keep stakeholders in the loop	**Conversation** Co-create the project with all those involved
Planning and scheduling Define work breakdowns, schedule and adjust activities	**Sense-making** An insightful model guides action when surrounded by uncertainty
Measuring and controlling Track progress on costs, risks, time and tasks	**Adaption** Adjust to ensure delivery occurs regardless of the changes

Figure 8.4: Complexity skills and characteristics

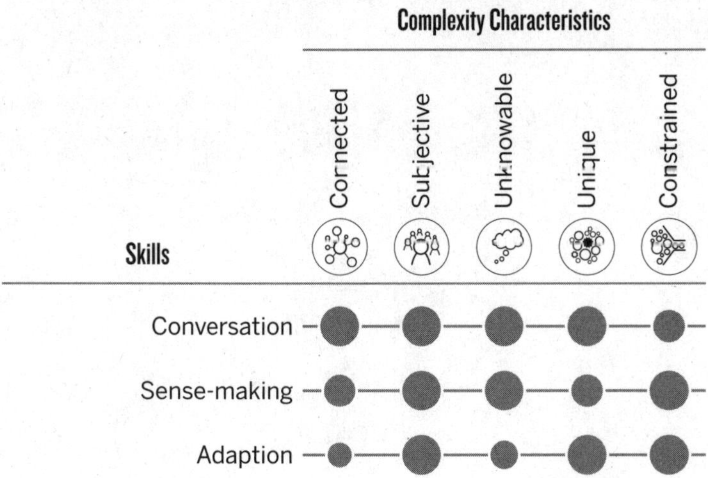

Chapter 9
MAKING IT HAPPEN

'You can't go back and change the beginning,
but you can start where you are and change the ending.'
—C.S. Lewis

The Complex Project Toolkit demands a different mode of thinking than the standard model of project management. The elements are different from the way most project managers operate. However, it's not enough to know that the Complex Project Toolkit is different; you need to be able to move to the new system, to build the mindsets and skills and implement the practices. As with any change, it takes time to learn a new language, internalise new ways of working and give up old habits.

Now that you know what is needed, what stands in the way of change? Where do you start, and how do you make it stick? This chapter is about how to give up the constantly reinforced habits of a lifetime. Because it is such a different way of thinking, the changes need to occur at all levels – individual, team and organisation – in order for them to be sustained. There will be resistance and a desire to stick with the current ways of operating. The most sustainable approach is to commit to the new way of working but start small, taking on new challenges with each project and building capability over time.

Start small

The first steps are the hardest. Once you start, and get a win or two, you and your team will build confidence. So, just get started.

For the first step, choose a change that:

1. impacts the project in a way that people will notice
2. is easy to implement
3. your team is willing to take on.

In one organisation I worked with, we introduced the Complex Project Toolkit on a single project. Their initial approach was to focus on the 'give up knowing' mindset and build capability in generative listening. They chose these elements because it was relatively easy to identify when they didn't do them well, and they could call out the wrong behaviour when they saw it. As they created a new language over time, the plan was to add more elements. Soon word got out about the new approach and other teams wanted to get involved. Another project ran an introductory session about the framework so they could pick up the elements that made sense for them and follow up with others later.

A good starting point for adopting the toolkit is to concentrate on the elements the team is drawn to. I've found that normally, the initial interest is in skills and mindsets. A common starting point for teams is to build capability in conversation skills, particularly developing listening abilities as a way to build connections and underpin the development of new practices. New mindsets reinforce these skills and can be supported with team operating principles, as discussed in the next section.

Regardless of how you start, trying to install the entire toolkit at once is unlikely to succeed because of the distraction caused as everyone tries to work out how to operate in the new world order. Taking on a couple of elements at a time and continuously reinforcing them is a more effective approach. The key is to find the pathway that works for you and your situation. This might be to build a baseline of skills across the board, or to focus on establishing new mindsets in a specific team. Taking on incremental improvements will lift performance in your complex projects.

Once you have made a start, plan out how to implement the rest of the Complex Project Toolkit. Expect to take a few months to become familiar with the ideas in this book and to internalise the concepts over the course of a few projects.

Build team performance

The project team is at the core of building and sustaining capability when taking on the Complex Project Toolkit.

The new skills and mindsets adopted by individuals have to be incubated in a supportive environment so they aren't killed off before they have a chance to take root. The project team is the greenhouse for this development. Project teams need sufficient autonomy to create their own 'micro-culture' that supports the growth of these new ways of working. Because the Complex Project Toolkit can be so different from the normal ways of operating, the project team must create an environment for experimentation where it is okay to try new things and build confidence over time. Start small and check in on progress regularly. You might begin with agreements on how to listen and 'hold space', or even just a willingness to check in on how people are feeling about the project. Over time, as everyone grows more confident in the power of the toolkit, it can expand into interactions with stakeholders and other teams.

A good place to start is by building operating principles and understanding individual capabilities.

Operating principles

Project teams can define principles that determine how they will operate within the project and interact outside the team. These are agreed ways of working that are reviewed regularly and reinforce behaviours, and can accelerate the development of mindsets, skills and practices.

I once worked with three teams on the same program. Each was given the option of setting up operating principles and having weekly check-ins against those principles. Two teams adopted this approach and one didn't. The team that didn't worry about operating principles got stuck into the project and progressed rapidly towards their objective. The other two teams spent time establishing how they would work together. After one month, the first team was racing ahead and getting things done. However, by the third month – when the initial enthusiasm wanes on most projects – there was an obvious shift. When things got tough, the teams that had taken the time to set up principles around how they would work improved their performance as the other project faltered.

Establishing effective operating principles can take a few iterations. Agreeing on the first round of principles can be done in a single meeting. For example, an operating principle could be 'to listen for the brilliance of others'. Another could be to 'seek first to understand', which anchors discussions on the topic rather than the individual putting it forward. This ensures contention is not avoided but actively sought as a method of learning. Whatever you choose, it is best to keep the list of principles short – less than ten – to begin with so they are simple to track. As you take a few minutes each week to check performance against these principles, you will find that some drop off because the team have internalised the activity, while others are replaced by a better version. Don't try to get them all right on the first go. Build something, check progress and let it evolve as the team grows.

Eventually the operating principles will develop into a language that makes communication fast, concise and clear. Individuals can call out ineffective behaviour or drive action with a single word or expression. Rituals also help to reinforce the new way of operating.

Individual capabilities

The individuals in the project team will have different backgrounds, skill-sets and thinking styles. Understanding these is essential when mapping out the path to building capability in the Complex Project Toolkit.

Are you better at divergent or convergent thinking? Are you able to expand ideas beyond the boundaries of the current topic, or are you better at extracting the significance of the situation? Do you like answers sooner, or are you willing to sit and distil ideas and change your mind as alternative insights emerge? Complex projects benefit from all types of thinkers, but they need to apply their skills at the right time in the project.

One of the things I have noticed when using designers on big projects is how different they are from technicians and project managers. They are very good at divergent thinking and creating objects, but projects can be high-pressure and conflict-rich environments. As mentioned previously, they are more comfortable in generative environments. It's a rare designer who enjoys an argumentative project delivery environment.

Conversely, imagine how hard it is for technicians to 'give up knowing', how hard it is for them to say, 'I don't know what I will find, but trust me to make it happen.' As a technician, how willing are you to go out on a limb because of what you believe, rather than just putting your trust in what you can prove? If you are over-reliant on convergent thinkers – people who know the answer and want to get moving – you run the real risk of rapidly delivering the wrong solution.

If you are a designer, be ready for the often-combative environment that can emerge and the potential for others to be frustrated by any lack of pace. If you are a project manager, open your heart to the possibility of more reflection and letting things emerge rather than rushing to an answer. Whatever your background and disposition, time and effort are required to build and sustain the skills required to operate well in complexity.

Bring a new style of leadership

Daniel Goleman, author of the 1995 bestseller *Emotional Intelligence*, teamed up with Richard Boyatzis and Annie McKee to define six leadership styles.[1, 2] Of the six, pacesetting is often valued in difficult projects because of the persistence in pushing forward. Pacesetting involves the leader driving to achieve results, setting very high standards for performance and pushing everyone to deliver as agreed. Anyone not keeping pace is asked to lift their performance or leave. While this might work in some complicated projects, it is dysfunctional in complex projects because it ignores the connected wickedness of the situation.

A combination of leadership styles is needed in complex projects. A collaborative style works best to increase the willingness and openness to learning while still maintaining focus on the outcome (as opposed to the plan). In complexity, it is important to create an environment in which people are willing to share and combine their ideas, to improve the flow of information and always move forward. Role clarity is important in ambiguity, but that doesn't mean you shouldn't share and listen to ideas. Keep in mind that the leadership style of the project is completely up to the program manager and the team. If you set up a project that makes it horrible for the people involved, then that is all on you. The culture of the project is not defined by some external force; it is a choice, and you have the ability to change it.

Persistence and resilience

One of the biggest changes of normal project management is the level of uncertainty. The emergent nature of complexity makes it very difficult to give people the certainty they might crave. Rather than just ignoring this or saying 'Cope with it', the complex project manager needs to build persistence and resilience in themselves and in their team.

Persistence is the willingness to keep moving even when there is no clarity. When you can't get an answer to a question, you don't give up – you go to the next person or department, pushing forward even when the action might feel futile.

Resilience goes hand in hand with this. Complexity and pushing through the fog can trigger a desire for things to be straightforward. The ever-changing nature of the situation, and being involved in something no one else has done yet, can cause you to question if you know what you are doing. Resilience is about being able to move forward and operate well in uncertainty despite feeling out of your depth.

Without persistence and resilience, the team is easily stopped when challenges arise. The opposite of persistence is resignation – giving in, believing the situation is too hard to handle. As a leader, the specific assistance you provide to each team member will depend on the individual, but overall it is about providing clarity of expectations, helping them realise that 'not knowing' is normal and being ready to respond when things go bad. It is about accepting that errors will occur and not criticising those who might have made the mistake. It is about maintaining focus on the end result and learning from every issue that arises.

Your ability to support the resilience of others will depend on your own comfort with ambiguity. You have to deal with any concerns you have before you can genuinely help others. In complexity, as with many other difficult things, it is helpful to have a mentor, or at least someone with whom you can discuss things and vent. You also need to balance the requirement to be the 'hard' project manager, delivering on deadlines and setting a high bar for performance, with the need to coach others through the uncertainty. Supporting the resilience of staff isn't always seen as the role of a project manager, but it is crucial both to delivering the project and to avoiding the injury these situations can cause individuals.

One of the signs to look for across the project is any form of resistance. Resistance can highlight disagreement, or it can be the result of misinterpretation. Either way, it is full of information, so it should be embraced. As a leader in complex projects adopting this new way of working, you need to combine the curiosity to keep learning with the courage of your convictions to address the underlying concerns.

Reinforce with the organisational environment

Transformation in the way we operate requires the whole community; it is not simply an individual journey. While teams can establish their own micro-culture with mindsets and practices for complexity, changes need to occur more broadly to promote and reinforce the changes. At an organisational level, this support comes down to two areas:

1. governance and decision-making that handles complexity
2. a culture and environment that support the new way of working.

Governance and decision-making

What does governance become in complex projects? How do you cope with the levels of unknowables when seeking approval? How do you approve something that you know, but can't easily prove, is valuable?

Given that in complex projects the plan is more of a thinking tool than a promise of performance, how does project tracking need to change? It can't just be about progress against budgets and plans when they were put together with incomplete information and don't survive the first contact with reality. Governance in the early stages of the project should focus on understanding the level of complexity that exists and testing the ability of the team to learn. No visible progress is fine if the understanding of the situation is improving and, as a result, the complexity is reduced.

In complexity, governance becomes more about identifying whether we are moving closer to or further away from the outcome. If we have learned something, do we still want to travel on this path? Is complexity increasing or falling? Is the project still worth it? Do we want to change the approach or abandon the attempt? Additionally, does what we have learned open up even more possibilities? If the governance process generates more questions, that isn't necessarily bad, so long as the project is not falling into the trap of diving into too much detail too early. Steering committees, a common form of governance, should be run as conversations addressing a different set of questions (see Table 9.1).

Table 9.1: Standard versus complex questions

Standard	Complex
Is the objective clear?	Have we asked the right questions?
Is the scope defined?	How have we named the problem?
Are we tracking to plan?	Do we need to change the approach?
Is the project structure in place?	Whose opinion is missing?
What are the explainable variances?	What have we learned?
What dependencies exist?	What wider impact will this create?
Are stakeholders managed?	Who else needs to know?

When it comes to decision-making in complexity, however much research you do, you will still need to make most calls without full knowledge. Many decisions in the early stages of complex projects are based on will and belief. Focus your effort on identifying which decisions will restrict future options and balance these with the cost of maintaining flexibility (by delaying decisions), realising that at some point you need to commit and move forward. Look for the 'no regret' decisions that would be made regardless of how the future reveals itself.

In the absence of proof, governance and decision-making in complexity is a search for resonance – for recurring messages and signs. In uncertainty you rarely move on just one piece of information; you need to see repetition in stories or data before you accept the pattern. This is about trusting your gut and understanding the difference between knowing you are doing the right thing and proving you are right (see Box N). Most people know the right thing to do but are held back because they are worried about the political implications or personal ramifications of a poor decision. This needs to be addressed at a cultural level.

Culture and environment

Along with governance, the culture and environment at play within the organisation impact the ability to sustain the Complex Project Toolkit. The ideal culture supports contention and learning, given their centrality to operating well in complexity. A good example of a learning focus is the 'just culture' found in aviation and heavy industries.

On the night of 22 December 2013, a British Airways 747 aircraft was taxiing for take-off from Johannesburg's OR Tambo International Airport. As it headed towards the end of the runway, it missed a turn, travelled down a small taxiway and the wing hit an office building. All 182 passengers and 17 crew were uninjured, but both the aircraft and the building sustained substantial damage. The subsequent investigation found that the pilots had not properly briefed the departure charts for the airport and had lost situational awareness.[3] However, the pilots were not fired for this transgression. The report also found a range of deficiencies in

N: Knowing versus proving

Knowing and proving are both valid forms of understanding, but they are not the same thing. I know I love my daughters, but I don't know how to prove it beyond doubt.

Proving is using external evidence to draw inferences that support a position. In projects it can be easier to focus on artefacts that are designed to support and prove the position, rather than on the essence of the situation. It is easier to show things being done by ticking off tasks on a Gantt chart or relying on an external review to confirm progress.

Knowing takes time and patience and experience, because it depends on the situation and your connection to it. Knowing includes the concepts of nous and intuition, trusting your gut.

Mark Strom identified five elements of knowing that provide insight for project managers:

1. All knowing is contextual.
2. All knowing is relational.
3. All knowing is a kind of immersion.
4. All knowing transforms us and what we do.
5. All knowing is more tacit than what we can list, explain, or even be aware of.[4]

As a project manager in complexity, you have to get close to the action, to immerse yourself in the frontline activities and environment so that you understand the context in which decisions are made. It is ineffective to make decisions in complex environments if you don't have a sense for how the wider system operates or the impact your actions will have on the individuals involved. Complexity is unique and can't be managed with a standard playbook that ignores the specific reality in this particular situation.

The governance model you establish in complexity has to create space to include knowing, not just proving where the project is at. Get into the project, walk around, ask questions and meet people. Look at the data, but also trust your instincts.

the navigation aids on the ground, including many taxiway lights not illuminated, unclear signage and no warning lights on the nearby buildings. A just culture understands that incidents and accidents have multiple causes, and provides the opportunity to learn and improve. It also knows that an investigation that seeks to apportion blame will guarantee that details remain hidden as a result of people's fear of recrimination. The openness of this investigation ensured that all the contributing factors were understood. If they had stopped at 'pilot error' as the cause, the improvements to lighting and marking would not have been made and it is likely that such an accident would have recurred.

Complex project managers need to create a similar open-dialogue and learning-focused culture that supports the ability to question the status quo and open up discussions. Such a culture also supports the resilience mentioned previously. Most people like certainty and comfort, but in complexity this is lacking. Any sense of threat based on lack of support in the uncertainty creates stress. This stress, in turn, can turn off the parts of the brain responsible for higher-order thinking at a time when it is most required.

The physical environment, including the setup of the facilities, also has a big impact on a project team's ability to operate in the new way. Most project managers know the value of co-location, even though it often isn't utilised. Beyond just locating the team, however, there are a range of constraints and signals in relation to the facility setup, and furniture in particular, that impact the way the team operates.

Here is a quick test. Look at the furniture in your office. Are the meeting rooms filled with rectangular tables with a whiteboard or display screen at one end? Do the chairs have fixed feet rather than rollers? Common meeting rooms with large tables and small whiteboards are designed for 'show and tell'. Complex projects operate better with more flexible furniture: large whiteboards or panels for displaying information, and movable tables and chairs that can be reconfigured to suit a conversation. As articulated by Kurt Lewin, 'Behaviour is a function of personality and environment.'[5]

However you choose to go about it, a new culture and environment is not something that can be forced on people. Everyone needs to be willing to take on the new way of operating; otherwise, it will evaporate quickly as the organisational antibodies defend the current way of working.

What stands in the way

Once you decide to implement a new operating model for complexity, as with any change, things get in the way. However, it isn't just about ensuring everyone follows a new process. It requires a shift in thinking, a change in the way people characterise the situation they see before them. Implementing the new toolkit runs up against many of the innate tendencies of people within an organisation – a love of certainty, underestimating complexity, not knowing the new rules and an impatience to get to the end. All of these tendencies can slow you down and send you running back to the familiar artefacts and known actions of the standard project management process.

Our love of certainty

How do you find certainty in complexity? You don't. That's the point. In fact, you never had it. Most people in complexity pretend to have it under control until they can quickly tame the situation (with the resulting loss of value); or, if that fails and the status plan goes red, then they reorganise, reset the project and probably fire someone.

Standard project management, even when things are going badly, can create the impression of certainty. It can be very difficult for people to give up their focus on control, particularly those who operate purely by the numbers, even if it has always been just an illusion. The Complex Project Toolkit is a new way of operating in which you lose that misguided sense of control, but you tackle the things that really need to be addressed – and, as a result, you have a much higher likelihood of a successful outcome.

Chasing certainty in complexity is like searching for the Holy Grail – a frustrating and fruitless quest that will ultimately lead to your destruction. The desire to tame situations prematurely, rather than sit with the wickedness, drives most of the problems described in Chapter 3.

If the project model you are working to is about minimising the level of change (a model preferred by anyone on a fixed-price contract) rather than embracing the emergence to create a better result, then you will continuously fight the shifting situation and be exhausted by that struggle, rather than being enlivened by the delivery of something significant.

Underestimating complexity

'It shouldn't be this hard' is a comment I have heard hundreds of times in projects from people unwilling to accept the level of complexity. This declaration is typical of the technician who believes there has to be one true answer. Another response that ignores the wickedness, as mentioned in Chapter 3, is, 'Everyone knows what to do, we just have to get on and do it.' Both of these statements are warning signs that you lack the capability, willingness or mindset to understand the level of complexity and deliver the project effectively.

Impatience to get there

Once people start on the transition to the Complex Project Toolkit, they want to get it over and done with quickly. This impatience to get through to the other side can cause the transition to be rushed and either not take hold or be abandoned before it has had a chance to succeed. Impatience can prompt people to shift what they do before they have completed the supporting change in thinking models. When the toolkit is applied without understanding the significance of the shift, it will not take hold. If it feels like it is taking too long to make the change, ask yourself if everyone believes the change is important.

Not knowing the new rules

One of the biggest issues when implementing a new system like the Complex Project Toolkit is that we don't know the rules of the new game. This applies to governance, benefits-tracking and planning. Even in the well-defined areas, people will arrive at different interpretations; it takes time to come to an agreement about what it means for your team in your organisation.

For example, I have talked about the fact that your plan is incorrect from the first day. Some might interpret this as suggesting you no longer need a plan in complexity. But complexity is not an excuse to completely ignore the activity of developing a plan. The plan represents the current thinking about how the project will play out. I had a plan when writing this book. Did I deliver on this first version of the plan? Not at all. Did it change much? Sometimes daily! Everything else going on in my life ensured that. Injuring my hand in a boating accident, which put me out of action for a couple of months, wasn't part of the plan. I changed the approach a number of times – from going about it chapter by chapter to drafting it all the way through and editing later. None of my plans were perfect, and some of them had no basis in reality. Each iteration of the plan represented a changing understanding of what it would take to complete all the pieces of the puzzle. But each plan helped me to maintain focus and keep moving forward. Having a poor plan is much better than having no plan because it shows you have put thought into what is going to happen.

Like taking on any change, this is really about comfort level. There's comfort in the existing approaches, and you're unsure what the new way of working should feel like or look like, whether you're doing it right or just doing what you're told. In times of stress, it is easy to revert to what you have done previously. It takes time to move to the new mindsets. It requires belief in their value and ownership of the journey to make them happen. You have to believe that you can learn this new way of working and that it is worthwhile.

My experience going from a scientific background to working in a design firm was uncomfortable, and I spent six months wondering what the heck was going on. But that's par for the course. That's the path you need to negotiate when you take on these new behaviours. It's not as simple as just picking up a new book. It takes commitment. It's hardly worth the journey if you don't believe it is possible or valuable to change.

Reinforce desirable patterns

There is a paradox in this discussion about how to go about implementing the Complex Project Toolkit. The rollout itself is complex and will require a different approach. You have to sense and respond to how these improvements go. In Kurtz and Snowden's paper on the Cynefin framework, they describe one situation in which they asked West Point graduates to manage the playtime of a kindergarten.[6] They were given time to prepare and they identified objectives, developed plans and backup strategies in case things didn't work out. As you can imagine, the result was chaos. What experienced teachers know to do is to let the session start and work to stabilise and reinforce desirable patterns and destabilise undesirable ways of interacting. Rolling out this toolkit is more like kindergarten playtime than military planning.

It is worth the effort

The Complex Project Toolkit introduces a new way of thinking about complex projects and a way of working that has proven successful across a range of situations, whether in accelerating a large-scale infrastructure design and build or redesigning the approach for a business transformation.

Taking on the toolkit – its mindsets, practices and skills – to add a new way of working to your project capability takes effort and commitment. It can be difficult to prove the benefit of the toolkit because there is no counterfactual data – there is no way of definitely showing how your project would have gone had the new approach not been in place.

I'm not suggesting you throw out everything you know. Rather, learn to recognise complexity, resist the urge to return to the security of the standard processes, surround yourself with a good team and extend their toolkit to drive improved project performance.

Start with one or two elements that draw you forward. Find a couple of projects whose teams want to try it out. Do it your way. You don't have to find the most complex project and force the new model onto others. The determination to keep trying, learning and improving will mark those who will move forward and deliver a new capability. Be impatient to build the capability, but don't let that impatience derail the effort as individuals and teams take on the new way of working.

You might not have the quantitative data to substantiate the improvement in the early stages, but you will hear it in the feedback you get from those close to the project. You will see it in issues being raised earlier, in fewer decisions being revisited or ignored, and in the increased commitment of the project team as they see their energy and effort being put to good use. The result will be a step change in complex project performance.

Conclusion

I started this book with the story of Sean and how his analysis showed that the large infrastructure project had a less than 1% chance of delivering the next major milestone on time. He saw that the probably of success had increased by spending time together as a team but wasn't able to explain it. Using design thinking, the approach was redesigned, relationships were improved, and new energy was brought to the team. Project performance was dramatically improved and it went on to deliver the significant milestone on time.

When I set out to write this book, my intent was to shift the thinking about project management and awaken readers to the reality that complex projects require a different response to normal. Experiences like the one with Sean have shown me that when project managers open up to a more connected and emergent approach, there is a significant improvement in performance. More importantly, the change in tactics improves the experience of those involved by reducing frustration and respecting their energy and commitment.

Achieving this outcome requires a recognition that the standard project toolkit is never going to be enough in complexity because it is built on an ineffective model of the world. The standard focus on planning, organising, staffing, directing and controlling comes from a different era and suits a different type of problem. This misalignment creates unproductive responses that lead to annoyance and hurt, not through malice but because of not knowing any better. No amount of strong processes and documentation will address the wicked and emerging social dimensions, or provide the certainty and control we crave.

It isn't enough to just call out the shortfalls of the existing methods. The shift in performance requires a new framing and a new narrative about how complex projects operate. The characteristics of complexity presented in Chapter 2 provide insight into how complex projects are different and why design thinking works as the foundational model. They elucidate how concepts such as connection and simplicity – not normally associated with project management – are fundamental to success in complexity.

However, success doesn't come from simply describing the new way of working: we need to alter the way we operate. The challenge is that we have a deep love of the existing toolkit because it has been successful in normal projects. Also, we have a love of certainty, both in business and personally, and the standard approach provides the appearance of certainty even where it doesn't exist. We want to know that the future will be okay, but that assurance can't be provided. To succeed in complexity, we have to give up on certainty and control. The trick is not to brace yourself in case things don't turn out as you planned, but rather to build the ability to respond when they don't. As Luke Skywalker says in *Star Wars: Episode VIII – The Last Jedi*, 'This is not going to go the way you think.'[7]

While there won't be certainty in complex projects, that doesn't mean you give up and become resigned to the situation. Complex projects are too important for that.

Delivering complex projects is worth your attention and the effort to get them right. Simple and complicated projects can be delivered with more certainty by seeking out best-practice experience, but anyone can do that. The real source of value in the future will be the ability to handle the wickedness of complex projects such as large-scale transformations or innovations. The most valuable projects have problems that are connected across organisational and industry boundaries, driven by individual perspectives, full of unknowables and distinguished by unique and constrained situations.

The ability to realise the value of your complex project, and not reduce your ambition to something that is demonstrably achievable, comes from taking on all elements of the Complex Project Toolkit. Bringing it all together – mastering the mindsets, learning the skills and executing the practices – will improve the likelihood of success and the experience of those involved. It represents a move towards a more human, creative and effective way of working in complexity.

All of this constitutes a significant change to your way of operating. It won't happen in a moment, because the siren call of certainty will keep dragging you back to the traditional project approach. Creating the new way of operating means a constant struggle between hope and reality – the hope of a future state and the reality of current pressures.

An essential element of moving to a new way of operating is a shift in the language. When terms such as 'sense and respond', 'give up knowing' and even 'lots of little explosions' start appearing as part of the normal course of business, you know the transition is underway.

My hope is that this book has opened up a new awareness and language for you – that it sparks a curiosity and drive to learn more, and an inability to ignore the nature of complexity and the problems of a purely mechanistic approach. I hope it creates a discomfort that makes you unwilling to put up with projects that sap energy and don't respect the effort of those involved. My desire is that, by embracing the Complex Project Toolkit and its new vocabulary, you will open up space for possibility and listening, and improve the overall experience of your projects. You will do away with ineffective responses and downward spirals into burnout. There will be more humanity, more engagement, more energy and a greater sense of belonging, of doing something significant. The Complex Project Toolkit gives you a path to turn what could be debilitating experiences into memorable acts of creation.

If your project is not working, have the courage to change it. The choice is yours. You get to decide how projects run. So, when it comes to complex projects, choose the right one, get it done, and make it fun. When you do this, you will be able to thrive and live well in complexity.

ABOUT THE AUTHOR

Kieran Duck has over 25 years' experience in running complex projects and transforming organisations, both as a consultant and as an executive responsible for delivery. He has redesigned and rescued multi-billion-dollar projects, and lead business transformations that open up new possibilities and ways of working for organisations and the people within them using the techniques outlined in this book.

He has presented globally on using design thinking to drive step changes in business transformations and has been a keynote speaker at offsites for companies looking to improve their strategy and program delivery performance. He has presented at university courses on project and change management.

Holding a Bachelor of Computer Science and a Master of Business Administration, Kieran has a strong analytical background. However, spending three years in a design firm opened up a whole new language and toolkit for him. Drawing upon that experience, he developed this unique approach to project management.

ACKNOWLEDGEMENTS

While many people have been involved in so many ways in creating this book, either providing a sounding board for the thoughts as they emerged or helping to refine the language, there were a few who stood out in their generosity and willingness to contribute. In the early days, Jeremey and Liam were willing to put up with the continuous, sometimes circular, debates as the ideas formed, and Fern always pushing me to get it down and finished. Greg had the patience to review the first full draft and Peter provided input on the final version. Tim provided guidance on the language of designers and David helped with the occasional roadblock in terminology. But through this whole process, no one stretched my thinking or was as willing to contribute to the development of the ideas as Nifeli. The thoughts in this book would also never have formed without her guidance and counsel. And final thanks go to Sharene for all the support and for keeping things running, Beth for drawings and design debates, Claire for discussions about mindsets and Grace for showing me what it means to be connected.

REFERENCES AND RESOURCES

Chapter 1: The evolution of project management

1. B Head & D Walker, 'The enormous cost of IT project failure', intheblack.com, 1 November 2016.
2. WM Bulkeley, 'A cautionary network tale: FoxMeyer's high-tech gamble', *The Wall Street Journal*, 18 November 1996.
3. Snowy Hydro, 'The Snowy Scheme', Snowy Hydro, viewed 3 May 2021, <snowyhydro.com.au/generation/the-snowy-scheme/>.
4. Destination Jindabyne, 'The history of Jindabyne', Destination Jindabyne, viewed 3 May 2021, <destinationjindabyne.com.au/history-of-jindabyne/>.
5. American Society of Civil Engineers (ASCE), 'Designated historic civil engineering landmarks', ASCE, viewed 3 May 2021, <web.archive.org/web/20070321063753/http://www.asce.org/history/landmark/projects.cfm>.
6. Engineers Australia, 'Snowy Mountains Hydro-Electric Scheme, 1949 to 1974', Engineers Australia, viewed 3 May 2021, <portal.engineersaustralia.org.au/heritage/snowy-mountains-hydro-electric-scheme-1949-1974>.
7. P Hunt, 'Snowy River deal delivers on its target 18 years on' *The Weekly Times*, 15 February 2017.
8. A Schiedel, 'Two of Dong Nai hydropower dams cancelled due to environmental concerns, Vietnam', *Environmental Justice Atlas*, 16 July 2015.
9. 'Hydro-power plans halted in Dong Nai', *Viet Nam News*, 1 October 2013.
10. E Ugarte, *Conquering complexity*, Helmsman Institute and University of Technology Sydney, Sydney, March 2015.
11. *Closing the Gap: designing and delivering a strategy that works*, Brightline Project Management Institute, Newtown Square, USA, 3 October 2017.

12. DH Pink, *A whole new mind; why right-brainers will rule the future*, Riverhead Books, New York, 2006.

Chapter 2: The nature of complexity

1. KB Hass & LB Lindbergh, 'The bottom line on project complexity: applying a new complexity model', paper presented at PMI® Global Congress 2010, Washington, D.C., October 2010.
2. JR Turner & RA Cochrane, 'Goals-and-methods matrix: coping with projects will ill defined goals and/or methods of achieving them', *International Journal of Project Management*, vol. 11, no. 2, May 1993, pp. 93–102.
3. *A framework for performance based competency standards for program managers*, Global Alliance for the Project Professions (GAPPS), 15 April 2011.
4. International Project Management Association (IPMA), 'The Certification Process in Detail', IPMA, viewed 11 May 2021, <www.ipma.world/individuals/certification/certification-process/>.
5. W Langewiesche, 'What really brought down the Boeing 737 Max?', *The New York Times Magazine*, 18 September 2019.
6. *Pulp Fiction* (1994).
7. HWJ Rittel & MM Webber, 'Dilemmas in a general theory of planning', *Policy Sciences*, vol. 4, 1973, pp. 155–169.
8. M Housel, 'The psychology of money', *Collaborative Fund*, 1 June 2018.
9. CF Kurtz & DJ Snowden, 'The new dynamics of strategy: sense-making in a complex and complicated world', *IBM Systems Journal*, vol. 42, no. 3, 2003, pp. 462–483.
10. DJ Snowden & ME Boone, 'A leader's framework for decision making', *Harvard Business Review*, November 2007.
11. G Larson, *The prehistory of The Far Side: a 10th anniversary exhibit*, Andrews McMeel Publishing, Kansas City, 1989.
12. JS Brown & P Dugold, 'Practice vs. process: the tension that won't go away', *Knowledge Directions: The Journal of the Institute for Knowledge Management*, Spring 2000, pp. 86–96
13. S Bradley, 'Why constraints are a fundamental part of design', Vanseo Design, 2 April 2015

Chapter 3: An incomplete toolkit

1. M Gladwell, *Blink: the power of thinking without thinking*, Little, Brown and Co, New York, 2005.

Chapter 4: We bought the wrong thinking model

1. FW Taylor, *The principles of scientific management*, Harper & Brothers, New York & London, 1911.
2. H Fayol, *General and industrial management*, Pitman, London, 1949.
3. L von Bertalanffy, *General system theory: foundations, development, applications*, George Braziller, New York, 1968.
4. C Higgins, 'How many combinations are possible using 6 LEGO bricks?' *Mental Floss*, 12 February 2017.
5. T Golsby-Smith, 'Pursuing the art of strategic conversations: an investigation of the role of the liberal arts of rhetoric and poetry in the business world', PhD thesis, 2001.
6. R Buchanan, 'Design and the new rhetoric: productive arts in the philosophy of culture', *Philosophy & Rhetoric*, vol. 34, no. 3, 2001, pp. 183–206.
7. M Strom, 'Decoding innovation and design (and how to make both happen)', LinkedIn, 18 March 2016.
8. T Brown, 'Design thinking', *Harvard Business Review*, June 2008.
9. J Liedtka, 'Why design thinking works', *Harvard Business Review*, September–October 2018.
10. J Liedtka, op. cit.
11. R Burch, 'Charles Sanders Peirce', *Stanford Encyclopedia of Philosophy*, 22 June 2001.
12. L March, 'The logic of design', *The Architecture of Form*, Cambridge University Press, Cambridge, 1976.
13. D Schon, *The reflective practitioner: how professionals think in action*, Basic Books, New York, 1982.

Chapter 5: A design-driven project toolkit

1. HWJ Rittel & MM Webber, op. cit.
2. Design Council, 'What is the framework for innovation? Design Council's evolved Double Diamond', Design Council, viewed 14 May 2021, <designcouncil.org.uk/news-opinion/what-framework-innovation-design-councils-evolved-double-diamond>.

Chapter 6: Mindsets for complexity

1. C Dweck, *Mindset: the new psychology of success*, Random House, New York, 2006.

2. J Kruger & D Dunning, 'Unskilled and unaware of it: how difficulties in recognizing one's own incompetence lead to inflated self-assessments', *Journal of Personality and Social Psychology*, vol. 77, 1999, pp. 1121–1134.
3. C Sagan, *The demon-haunted world: science as a candle in the dark*, Random House, New York, 1995.
4. N Clark, 'The Airbus saga: crossed wires and a multibillion-euro delay' *The New York Times*, 11 December 2006.
5. D Rock, 'Managing with the brain in mind', *Strategy+business*, 27 August 2009.
6. KM Eisenhardt & JA Martin, 'Dynamic capabilities: what are they?', *Strategic Management Journal*, vol. 21, no. 10–11, pp. 1105–1121.
7. CC Mann, *The wizard and the prophet: two remarkable scientists and their dueling visions to shape tomorrow's world*, Alfred A Knopf, New York, 2018.

Chapter 7: Effective practices in complexity

1. YN Harari, *Sapiens: a brief history of humankind*, Harper, New York, 2015.
2. R Weiss, 'The opposite of addiction is connection: new addiction research brings surprising discoveries', *Psychology Today*, 30 September 2015.
3. S Jones et al., '10 of the best words in the world (that don't translate into English)', *The Guardian*, 27 July 2018.
4. B Cahill, 'When collaboration meets competition: the real lessons from the Dutch Open Hackathon', Philips, viewed 3 May 2021, <philips.com/a-w/about/news/archive/blogs/innovation-matters/when-collaboration-meets-competition-the-real-lessons-from-the-dutch-open-hackathon.html>
5. F Chung, 'Why Amazon executives dread the "question mark" email from Jeff Bezos', news.com.au, 27 April 2018.
6. 'Rhetological fallacies: errors and manipulation of rhetoric and logical thinking', Information Is Beautiful, viewed 3 May 2021, <informationisbeautiful.net/visualizations/rhetological-fallacies/>.
7. C Sagan, op. cit.
8. J Kolko, 'Abductive thinking and sensemaking: the drivers of design synthesis', *Massachusetts Institute of Technology Design Issues, vol. 26, no. 1, Winter 2010, pp. 15–28.*

9. G McKeown, *Essentialism: the disciplined pursuit of less*, Crown Business, New York, 2014.
10. C Thorpe & S Shapin, 'Who was J. Robert Oppenheimer? Charisma and complex organization', *Social Studies of Science*, vol. 30, no. 4, 2000, pp. 545–590.
11. C Thompson, 'How being bored out of your mind makes you more creative', *Wired*, 25 January 2017.
12. J Odell, *How to do nothing: resisting the attention economy*, Melville House, New York, 2019.
13. National Aeronautics and Space Administration, U.S.A., 'SP-4209 the partnership: a history of the Apollo-Soyuz Test Project', NASA, viewed 17 May 2021, <https://www.hq.nasa.gov/office/pao/History/SP-4209/ch3-6.htm>.
14. N Stewart, *Enabling systemic conversations: exploring the role of design in strategy implementation*, RMIT University, 2012.
15. J Hobson, 'How New Orleans reduced its homeless population by 90 percent', WBUR, 19 February 2019.
16. T Swart, 'Study into the mental resilience of journalists', taraswart.com, May 2017.
17. D Ariely, E Kamenica & D Prelec. 'Man's search for meaning: the case of Legos', *Journal of Economic Behavior & Organization*, vol. 67, no. 3–4, 2008, pp. 671–677.
18. D DeNicola, 'You don't have a right to believe whatever you want to', *Aeon*, 14 May 2018.
19. J Stengel, *Grow: how ideals power growth and profit at the world's greatest companies*, Crown Business, New York, 2011.

Chapter 8: Enhanced project skills

1. D Whyte, *Crossing the unknown sea: work as a pilgrimage of identity*, Riverhead Books, New York, 2001.
2. M Strom, *Grounded questions. Rich stories. Deep change*, TEDxPlainpalais, YouTube, uploaded 27 March 2013.
3. E de Bono, *Six thinking hats*, Little, Brown and Co, Boston, 1985.
4. JH Larkin & HA Simon, 'Why a diagram is (sometimes) worth ten thousand words, *Cognitive Science*, vol. 11, no. 1, 1987, pp. 65–100.
5. B Nease, 'How your brain keeps you believing crap that isn't true', *Fast Company*, 31 August 2016.
6. D Roam, *The back of the napkin: solving problems and selling ideas with pictures*, Portfolio, New York, 2008.

7. GR Rodriguez, 'This is your brain on storytelling: the chemistry of modern communication', *Forbes*, 21 July 2017.
8. PJ Zak, 'Why your brain loves good storytelling', *Harvard Business Review*, 28 October 2014.
9. K Smith, *How to be an explorer of the world: portable life museum*, TarcherPerigee, New York, 2008
10. CF Chabris & DJ Simons, *The invisible gorilla: and other ways our intuitions deceive us*, Crown, New York, 2010.
11. SL Beckmann & M Barry, 'Innovation as a learning process: embedding design thinking', *California Management Review*, vol. 50, no. 1, Fall 2007, pp. 25–56.
12. DH Pink, op. cit.
13. B Minto, *The pyramid principle: logic in writing and thinking*, Financial Times Prentice Hall, London, 1987.
14. R Moss Kanter, 'Managing yourself: zoom in, zoom out', *Harvard Business Review*, March 2011.
15. W Duggan, *Strategic intuition: the creative spark in human achievement*, Columbia University Press, New York, 2007.
16. J Useem, 'The long-forgotten flight that sent Boeing off course', *The Atlantic*, 20 November 2019.
17. B Burnett & D Evans, *Designing your life: how to build a well-lived, joyful life*, Alfred A Knopf, New York, 2016.

Chapter 9: Making it happen

1. D Goleman, R Boyatzis & A McKee, *Primal leadership: realizing the power of emotional intelligence*, Harvard Business School Press, 2002.
2. R Benincasa, '6 leadership styles and when you should use them', *Fast Company*, 29 May 2012.
3. S Hradecky, 'Accident: British Airways B744 at Johannesburg on Dec 22nd 2013, took wrong taxiway and buried wing in building', *Aviation Herald*, 23 December 2013.
4. M Strom, 'Knowing is bigger than thinking', link no longer active, <markstrom.co/knowing-is-bigger-than-thinking/>
5. A Sharma, 'Why mindset is overrated in behavior change', LinkedIn, 19 July 2017.
6. CF Kurtz & DJ Snowden, op. cit.
7. *Star Wars: Episode VIII – The Last Jedi* (2017)

INDEX